Soundings

Issue 11

Emotional Labour

EDITORS
Stuart Hall
Doreen Massey
Michael Rustin

GUEST EDITOR
Pam Smith

POETRY EDITOR
Carole Satyamurti

REVIEWS EDITORS
Becky Hall and
Susanna Rustin

ART EDITOR
Tim Davison

EDITORIAL OFFICE
Lawrence & Wishart
99a Wallis Road
London E9 5LN

MARKETING CONSULTANT
Mark Perryman

ADVERTISEMENTS
Write for information to Soundings,
c/o Lawrence & Wishart

SUBSCRIPTIONS
1999 subscription rates are (for three issues):
UK: Institutions £70, Individuals £35
Rest of the world: Institutions £80, Individuals £45

ISSN 1362 6620
ISBN   0 85315 890 8

Text setting Art Services, Norwich
Cover photograph: ©   Dympna Casey

Printed in Great Britain by
Cambridge University Press, Cambridge

Soundings is published three
times a year, in autumn,
spring and summer by:
Soundings Ltd
c/o **Lawrence & Wishart**
99a Wallis Road
London E9 5LN

CONTENTS

Continued on next page

Continued from previous page

NOTES ON CONTRIBUTORS

Frances Angela was born in 1950, and lives in London with her partner and son. She started writing poetry in her mid-forties, and has been published in various magazines.

Les Back, Tim Crabbe and **John Solomos** are currently engaged in a research project, The Cultures of Racism in Football. The essay they contribute in this issue is drawn from a book that will be published by Berg in 1999 entitled *The changing face of football: racism, multiculture and identity in the English game.*

Dympna Casey is Lecturer in the Centre for Nursing, National University of Ireland, Galway.

Prue Chamberlayne is Director, Centre for Biography in Social Policy (BISP), University of East London.

Gillian Clarke is a poet and author of *Selected Poems* (Carcanet 1985).

Christine Clegg is a tutor in English and Cultural and Community Studies at the University of Sussex.

Phil Cohen is Director of the Centre for New Ethnicities Research at the University of East London. He is author of *Rethinking the Youth Question* (1997).

David Goldblatt teaches politics at the Faculty of Social Sciences at the Open University.

Andreas Hess teaches sociology at the University of Wales, Bangor. He is currently working on a book, *American Social and Political Thought.*

Stephen Lloyd Smith is Lecturer in Management Studies, Brunel University.

Rosy Martin is a photographer, writer, workshop leader, counsellor and designer.

Marjorie Mayo is Reader in Professional and Community Education (Pace), Goldsmiths College, University of London.

Minoo Moallem is Assistant Professor of Women's Studies, San Francisco State University.

Dorothy Nimmo has been an actress, wife-and-mother, goatherd, cook and gardener. Her most recent volume of poetry, *The Children's Game*, was a Poetry Book Society Recommendation.

Kevin Parry was born in Umtata, South Africa and has been living in England since 1979. He has won a number of short story prizes and recently completed his first collection.

T.V. Sathymurthy was a leading authority on Indian democracy. His edited four-volume study *Social Change and Political Discourse in India* was published by Oxford University Press in 1996. He taught for thirty years in the politics department at the University of York. He died in 1998.

Pam Smith is Professor of Nursing at South Bank University. She is the author of *The Emotional Labour of Nursing* (Macmillan 1992).

Sue Williams is Senior Lecturer, Faculty of Health, South Bank University.

Frances Wilson teaches, writes and paints. Her collection of poetry, *Close to Home*, is published by Rockingham Press.

Michael Young does not regard himself as a professional poet. Some of his poems, and those of his wife, Sasha Moorsom, were published as a book, *Your Head in Mine* (Carcanet, 1994). He is a sociologist and social entrepreneur.

A Third Way with teeth

Last autumn saw a great flurry of debate about the direction of New Labour, both from the advocates of its 'Third Way', and from its sharpest critics yet, the authors of 'Wrong', the one-off issue of *Marxism Today*. However, those who hoped that these interventions would begin a reflective discussion of where 'the Project' was headed, well into Labour's first term of office, were quickly in for disappointment. In the United States, where a well-publicised seminar on the Third Way had taken place between President Clinton, Tony Blair and their advisors, Clinton was soon facing impeachment. In Britain, the resignations from office of Peter Mandelson, Geoffrey Robinson and Charlie Whelan have revealed deep antagonisms at the centre of the New Labour project (although one needs the skills of a Kremlinologist to decipher what if any ideological or programmatic significance these differences may have).

New Labour's 'Third Way' was described recently as a brand-image in search of a product. Its rapid fade from the headlines, and lack of intellectual substance, suggests that this description has considerable truth. In fact, there have been at least two previous 'Third Ways' in the history of the left, and it has not added to enlightenment that this new version has presented itself as if it were entirely new-born. Examining New Labour's relationship to earlier 'Third Ways' can give an insight into its current practices.

Third Way 1: Social democracy

The first of these 'third ways' was social democracy itself, which emerged in the 1880s as a parliamentary, or democratic, alternative to authoritarian socialism, or Communism. The mainstream of social democracy aimed throughout its history to limit and complement the productive powers and energies of capitalism via a democratic state, taxation, a mixed economy (usually with a substantial public sector), strong trade unions, welfare guarantees, and a commitment to a measure of equality. Edouard Bernstein, Anthony Crosland, and John Kenneth Galbraith, with his ideas of 'private affluence and public squalor', and 'countervailing powers', were leading exponents of this tendency. The right-wing version of this tradition was prepared to settle for a mixed economy, and for a long-term balance between state and market, private and public sectors, democracy and capitalism. It wished to balance, not sacrifice, the benefits of free markets, and was fearful of excessive state or trade union power.

The left-wing version of democratic socialism was more ambitious, and aimed for the long-run abolition of capitalism by democratic means. This was the intention signified by Clause 4 of the Labour's Party's constitution, setting as a distant objective the common ownership of the means of production and distribution. An enlarged public sector, industrial democracy, and the Swedish wage-earner fund proposals in the 1970s, were means to achieve these ends. Arguments about how far and how fast to go along this road were central dividing issues between left and right in the Labour Party, over several generations. The idea of 'stakeholding', promoted most effectively by Will Hutton, is a recent attempt to give new life to this argument, proposing to create more democratic forms of governance of capital whilst accepting the benefits of markets and a continuing dominant role for private share-ownership.

The advocates of the New Labour 'Third Way' have defined their project against a particular form of social democracy - Keynesianism, corporatism, 'the welfare state as we know it', and the male breadwinner family - equating the whole social democratic tradition with the specific forms it adopted in the post-war period, and especially with the failures of the Labour Party in the 1960s and 1970s. But while New Labour formulations establish a convenient definition of 'modernisation' as that which is not 'Old Labour', they misrepresent the essence of social democracy. This insisted, in both its right and left wing variants, on the fact that capitalism generated systemic problems, of inequality and instability, and that the primary task of social democracy was to confront these holistically. Without capitalism as one of its antagonists, the idea of social democracy would have had no meaning.[1]

New Labour does of course address issues in the real world, even if the proscriptions of 'Old Labour' ways of speaking restrict its vocabulary for talking about them. Whereas social democracy used to present itself as a countervailing force to the market, the Third Way positions itself mid-way between 'neo-liberalism', whose excesses are to be curbed, and the abuses of government. The New Right turned attention away from 'market failure' to 'non-market failure' (ie failures of the state and of collective provision). It has been one of the worst legacies of Thatcherism that New Labour has continued in the same vein. It is far more critical of the problems of social democracy than it is of capitalism. The development of an 'active labour market' policy to increase employability, via education, and training - which should be a complement to reducing inequality via the tax system as in Sweden - is instead presented as its 'modern' alternative; the endemic tendency of markets to generate cumulative inequalities is redefined as the problem of social exclusion; it is noted that the irresponsible powers of private capital have globalised themselves, and Anthony Giddens in his book The Third Way says that something must be done about this; the government has an environmental policy, but the systemic connections between global market forces and environmental risk are not identified.

New Labour thus constructs a piecemeal debate about the local (or global) excesses of the market system without acknowledging that these problems are systemic, and that alternative forms of power must be asserted, if only as counter-balances to capital. Since in its depleted and confusing theoretical landscape, nothing is meaningfully connected to anything else, its political outcome can only be pragmatism. We have 170 manifesto commitments, but what model of society, and of the balance of power within it, their fulfilment would amount to, no-one can say. Thus, in identifying a particular form of social democracy as its only possible form, New Labour has deprived itself of a crucial part of its critical armoury.

Third Way 2: The New Left

The second of the 'Third Ways' in whose shadow the new version exists is

---

1. Chantal Mouffe in *Soundings* 9 criticised the emptiness of a politics without antagonisms.

the 'New Left', which defined itself, from its beginnings in 1956, against Stalinism on the one hand, and Fabian social democracy on the other. This connection has been valuably made by Mark Perryman and Anne Coddington in their introduction to *The Moderniser's Dilemma,* a useful and forward-thinking collection of essays on these issues.[2] The politics of the new left were defined as anti-capitalist, but also as anti-bureaucratic and anti-statist. The new left was also the first political formation to identify a post-materialist and thus modern political agenda, which included among other issues the 'quality of life', the meaning of work, democratic self-activity, and the creation of an expressive and democratic culture. The new left had several phases of development, which encompassed an anti-nuclear internationalism (another 'Third Way' between the two poles of the Cold War), the idea of a cultural politics, a renewal of Marxism as a flexible theoretical perspective, the turn to feminism, and the lasting emergence of a radical presence in many academic disciplines - for example as popular history, in a theoretically-informed social and cultural geography, and in the emergence of cultural studies. Perry Anderson perceptively described these developments as 'a culture in contraflow', pointing to the paradox that an enriching of radical intellectual and cultural life continued right through a long period of political defeat, in the 1980s and 1990s. Successive moments in this new left trajectory were the foundation of the *New Reasoner* and *Universities and Left Review,* their merger as *New Left Review* and its own subsequent, transmutations, *The May Day Manifesto, Beyond the Fragments,* and *Marxism Today.* Through the GLC, this tradition became briefly a part of government.

The most direct influence of this tradition on the New Labour project came from *Marxism Today,* and it is this which explains some of the bitterness of the MT authors towards the misappropriation of their contribution to the left's renewal. 'New Times', MT's own brand-image for a reconstructed though still socialist politics, was cousin or ancestor to New Labour. However, those who spent their youth in waving the banners of the politics of the young - this is what the label 'new' usually signifies - must not complain too much when they too are eventually cast into the camp of the

---

2. Anne Coddington and Mark Perryman (eds), *The Moderniser's Dilemma,* Lawrence and Wishart, London 1998.

outmoded. As the New Left constructed the Old as its imaginary other, so New Labour has defined 'Old Labour', though without the commitment to dialogue and continuity which were fundamental to the new left, from its early days of revisionist and dissident Communism in the 1950s onwards.

What New Labour has taken from the 'New Times' position is an insistence on the need for a new political project - and new vocabularies and images for this - a rejection of merely statist or as we might also now say 'Fordist' programmes, a critique of simplistic class-politics, an attention to feminist agendas, and a commitment to democratic renewal, via constitutional reform. The 'post-material' agendas of environmental conservation, and attention to cultural meaning and expressive style are also part of the package.

It has however been a very selective appropriation.[3] Perhaps its deepest weakness has been its rejection of the intellectual heritage not only of social democracy, but of the new left too. It seems to be impossible to construct a serious debate about alternative futures, about the limits of what is possible (arguments within democratic socialism have always concerned the limits of the possible, in electoral and other ways), about how programmes and policies might conceivably be different from what they are. The significance of Geoff Mulgan's attack on the irrelevance of academics in the special *Marxism Today* is its virtual dismissal of theoretical argument itself. The MT issue plainly wounded some feelings, but its invitations to open debate have not been taken up.[4]

One reason for this failure to engage in debate is that New Labour has adopted a quite different model of politics. The New Left sought to go beyond a politics that was merely electoral, or 'psephological' as Edward Thompson used to say, and was identified with the new social movements from CND onwards; but New Labour has decided that the electoral is more or less everything. Politics has never been more professional, and the professionalism that counts, and which represents the most innovative dimension of the project, comes from the field of marketing. The Clintonisation of Labour, which we described in an earlier editorial, has meant taking from the New Democrats in the United States a 'super-realism' of the political marketplace. What matters

---

3. On this see articles by Michael Kenny in *Soundings* 6, and Alan Finlayson in *Soundings* 10.
4. The personal rivalries that seem so pervasive in this government, and which have found semi-public expression through press briefings etc, are a destructive substitute for disallowed political debate.

is to construct a political product that will sell, and to sell it unrelentingly. With Clinton's difficulties, and now the fall of Peter Mandelson - the whiz-kid of the new professionalism - the wheels have fallen off this vehicle unexpectedly quickly. The current crisis of New Labour has exposed how dependent its project is on its presentational strategies. What else, after all, is it about? What values, beliefs, long-term purposes, enduring alliances, can it call upon to sustain itself through difficult times? A broader concept of politics is called for.

So far, in fact, three things have happened in response to New Labour's current difficulties. The first was a flurry of somewhat contentless statements by Prescott et al implying some revival of 'basic' commitments of a social democratic kind. The second was the announcement of a campaign of concerted speeches, led off by the Prime Minister, to restate the New Labour script. This 'reiterating the message' approach was reminiscent of the Major years, where innumerable relaunches of this kind took place, all presupposing that the political problem was in communication, not substance. One was just thinking that the Thatcherites - real strategists of hegemony they - would have acted differently, and dreamed up some new idea to push forward their permanent revolution, and to locate new enemies on the other side, when the third response appeared. Blair (in South Africa, of all places) and Blunkett announced their plan to take failing schools into private ownership![5] Is the New Labour project to take the Thatcher privatisation programme even further than the Iron Lady did herself?

Arguments which attempt to maintain some connections between New Labour and these earlier attempts to define a 'Third Way' have been important to *Soundings*, and we will continue to make them. It does however become wearying to see serious arguments, like those of the *MT* special issue, dismissed just because they remain connected to earlier socialist debate. We are therefore going to propose some new areas of discussion, by focusing on the Third Way as those close to New Labour, such as Demos, define it. We are going to explore the idea of an enlarged social space which is genuinely distinct from both market and state.

---

5. Sally Tomlinson's article 'Education dilemmas in a post-welfare society', *Renewal* Vol. 6 No. 3, 1998, explains lucidly the extreme contradictions of contemporary education policy, in which the competitive struggle for positional advantage by middle-class parents in fact dominates policy, and the relative disadvantage made inevitable by this is blamed on 'failing schools' and their teachers.

Third Way 3: Giving substance to the social

David Marquand, in a recent pamphlet, pointed out the huge opportunity for a lasting political realignment that has been seized by New Labour.[6] The idea of reuniting the traditions of collectivist liberalism and social democracy, after a hundred years of division, and of casting the Conservatives into marginality, is not to be lightly dismissed. Labour constitutional reforms are the most robust elements in its strategy of realignment,[7] but Marquand rightly points out that these are not enough. He looks, as New Labour itself has done, to an amplified idea of 'the social' as a way of building a larger progressive coalition. The problem is to know what substantive meaning can be given to this idea, especially if, for Blair though not for Marquand, the destructive aspects of capitalism are excluded from the debate.

In the Blairite Third Way, 'the social' denotes a terrain - elsewhere described as 'civil society' - lying somewhere between the market and the state.[8] The idea of social responsibility has always been a distinctive theme of Tony Blair's own speeches.[9] Through this he has sought to identify a politics that is not Thatcherite - competitive, individualist, callous, etc - but is not statist or collectivist either. This emphasis on the social rather than the socialist has indicated the affinities of Blair's politics with a collectivist Liberal, Christian tradition, rather than with the more materialist framework of socialism. (There are strong affinities between Blair's visceral anti-Marxism and the founding culture of European Christian Democracy.)

We can usefully distinguish the social from other forms of organisation.

---

6. David Marquand, *Must Labour Win?*, Fabian Society, 1998.
7. Andrew Gamble argues this case compellingly in *The Moderniser's Dilemma*.
8. In authoritarian regimes, civil society has been taken to mean everything outside the control of the state. But in societies where power is mostly divided between powerful corporations and government, it is better to define civil society independently of corporate power.
9. E.g.: 'By contrast, socialism as defined by certain key values and beliefs is not merely alive, it has historic opportunity now to give leadership. The bases of such socialism lies in its view that individuals are socially interdependent human beings - that individuals cannot be divorced from the society to which they belong. It is, if you will, social-ism.' Tony Blair, *Socialism*, Fabian pamphlet 565, 1994; and, 'Human nature is cooperative as well as competitive, selfless as well as self-interested, and society could not function if it were otherwise. We all depend on collective goods for our independence, and all our lives are enriched - or impoverished - by the communities to which we belong.' Tony Blair, *The Third Way*, Fabian pamphlet 588, 1998.

The American sociologist Amitai Etzioni (one of the inspirers of communitarianism) in his early work distinguished between coercive, instrumental, and normative organisations.[10] Coercive organisations obtain compliance through sanctions, instrumental organisations win compliance through material and other rewards, and normative organisations gain compliance from identification, altruistic commitment, and moral belief. The institutions which broadly correspond to these are prisons and armies (the coercive), firms operating in the market (the instrumental), and families, churches, and voluntary associations (the normative). In practice all organisations make some use of each of these forms of compliance, and considerable boundary-crossing takes place. Military units give great importance to morale and solidarity, firms have command structures, churches and voluntary organisations operate (increasingly) in the market place. But the broad distinction seems clear.

What would be involved in extending the scope of this normative or 'social' form of organisation and relatedness in late capitalism? It would require a lessening of the domination of society by the institutions of both the market and state. It would also mean moving towards more value-oriented, humanly-respectful, and communicative modes of co-operation *within* the market and state sectors. It would require opening up an agenda of debate about goals and values beyond those of consumption and personal enrichment. Such a programme really would amount to a 'Third Way'.

The practical limit of New Labour aspiration thus far seems to be that Gross National Product will rise in a consistent way by two or three per cent each year, and that it will become possible to provide decent welfare services within a roughly constant balance between public and private expenditures. In other words, the social good is equated largely with rising personal consumption, so long as a basis of social entitlements, more generally available employment, and some enhancement of political citizenship are achieved. This vision might even encompass some degree of surreptitious redistribution, if Labour stayed in office long enough.

There may however be the beginnings of recognition that the New Labour project needs a concept of ends and values which goes beyond a more inclusive

---

10. A. Etzioni, *A Comparative Analysis of Complex Organisations*, Free Press 1961.

version of consumer capitalism. David Marquand's pamphlet, a Demos collection entitled *The Good Life*[11], and a recent speech by John Prescott on quality of life indices, have recently raised these issues in suggestive ways, though with few practical recommendations.

The major traditions of political theory each pay at least formal homage to the idea of intrinsic goals and satisfactions, placing these above and beyond the merely instrumental or selfish. Conservatives, like Roger Scruton today, give weight to values embedded in tradition and continuity. Liberals, like Mill or Berlin, give their emphasis to individual self-development and its achievements. The concept of the social has always been crucial for socialists. The socialist imaginary was of co-operative, social activities, pursued for their own sake. Marx's hope of abolishing involuntary labour, William Morris's world of artisan self-expression, Raymond Williams's democratic culture; each envisaged a world beyond materialism and self-interest. This is also the significance of Michael Walzer's various 'spheres of justice'. These are fields of intrinsic or social satisfaction, such as are obtained in many relationships of family and friendship, in institutions which depend on voluntary commitment, on callings - even the production of little magazines - which people pursue mainly for enjoyment or out of belief. One of the reasons why the public becomes identified with professional sports stars, or musicians (as in Radio 3's 'Artists of the Week' or 'Private Passions') is because their working lives have dimensions of expressive as well as material satisfaction, dimensions which many working lives don't have to this extent.

Socialism always envisaged that this sphere of altruistic activity would grow, and the sphere based on coercion and acquisition would eventually diminish. It was in this spirit that the GLC sought to devolve resources to varieties of community groups. The plans for the recycling of domestic waste that are being developed by Robin Murray for example, following many Continental and North American precedents, which ask householders to sort their domestic waste carefully into different containers for recycling, have an ethical and an aesthetic, as well as practical dimension, imagining domestic waste recycling as a kind of social education in sustainability. And there is no purpose in a magazine such as *Soundings* if no future can be envisaged beyond that of the acquisitive and consumer society.

---

11. Ian Christie and Linda Nash (eds), *The Good Life*, Demos 1998.

Expanding the social sector

New Labour's own gestures towards the values of the social have not so far been very enticing. They have been more directed towards remoralising the poor and deviant than towards a new version of the good society. There seems to be an idea that greater social connectedness can be achieved by moral preaching. Geoff Mulgan has argued that the role for new-style government should be to set moral agendas, to shape minds rather than change institutions.

Such institutional strategy as there has been has focused on the deficiencies of the public sector, not on market failures. But even in the public sector what has usually been proposed has been more regulation and competition, with methods often based on adopted and already-outmoded models of business management. Recent government proposals to improve services to children in care resort primarily to coercive regulation, not to investment in better training or to more reflective institutional practices. 'Failing schools' are now liable to be taken over by private companies; it is a long time since we heard the countervailing suggestion that failing private firms, however important the public needs which they serve, should be taken into the public sector. The suspicion of 'producer interests', whether of professionals or trade unions, sits ill with the idea that services depend on the dedication, skill and capacity to learn of their workforces. Rather than moving the public sphere in democratic and normative directions, New Labour policy is continuing to force it towards the norms of business. What should be expected of a centre left government is that it be at the very least objective and impartial between the claims of state and market, but this is not New Labour's position.

Meanwhile the private sector's contribution to the development of the social sphere is meant to come from the spirit of 'partnership'. There are, however, severe limits on the extent to which private firms in the market, governed by overriding pressure to make money for their shareholders (at present their only stakeholders), can afford to divert resources to social goods. Firms that went far down this road would risk jeopardising their position in competition with those who don't, 'free riders' as far as social benefits are concerned. If 'partnership' is to become more than a pious and often hypocritical ideal, some different framework of corporate obligations is needed.

We think there needs to be a rebalancing of the scale of private, public, and voluntary or non-profit sectors, and a significant strengthening of the third of these. The relative weight of non-profit agencies might be taken as one index of the strength of civil society, and of social wellbeing. A tangible measure of the strengthening of the non-profit sector would be the increase in the proportion of national resources which it disposed of during New Labour's term of office. This sector currently accounts for about 4 per cent of employment in the economy. One might aim to see its size double over a period of a decade.

This would require decisive government action, not (only) in 'old' social democratic mode to tax and spend resources through its own agencies, but instead to ensure that national resources are devolved to self-active associations of many kinds, operating under a regulatory regime which would have to be developed from present charity law.

Hitherto, such resources as have gone to 'the voluntary sector' (for example, housing associations) have largely been redistributed from what was previously public, usually local authority provision. The resources have come ultimately from individual taxation. The culture of 'contracting out' of public services has increased provision by non-profit, and profit-making, organisations. This has had the effect of reorganising existing public provision, in the context of its quasi-marketisation, not of a rebalancing of private and public provision. It has been at the expense of the public, not the market sector.

We propose something quite different. This is that private corporations of above a specified turnover should be required to devote a proportion of their pre-tax profits (e.g. one per cent rising eventually to five per cent) to the social good. To meet this requirement, firms would be obliged to contribute this resource to organisations, which they would choose, but which would be recognised and regulated by law as charities. This could include agencies which firms could themselves set up as charitable agencies. There is no good reason to deny firms the reputational credit of association with 'good works' that they might directly organise and sponsor, as many socially progressive firms already do. There is every reason why corporate decisions about the disbursement of such funds should be made jointly by employees as well as managers and shareholders.

The Charities Aid Foundation recently reported in its 'Generosity Index' that the average corporate contribution to charity as a proportion of pre-tax profits is a meagre 0.22 per cent. All but two of the largest ten corporate givers, in absolute terms, give less than 0.7 per cent of pre-tax profits to charitable purposes. It is clear that compulsion on firms to contribute to social goods in this way would make a substantial difference to the resources available for the non-profit sector.[12]

How could such a radical step be justified? Why should even a small proportion of shareholders profits be appropriated in this way? The reason is that the ownership of capital should involve some social obligations and responsibilities. Although this is currently recognised in the liability to capital taxation, there are good 'Third Way' arguments why even elected governments should not have monopolistic control over all social goods, and why responsibilities for them should be more widely diffused. What an obligation of this kind would do is to impose on all substantial companies responsibilities already voluntarily accepted by the best.

A second reason for this proposal is of course the great social and community benefits that could be expected. The voluntary sector would be immeasurably strengthened by the large increase in its material resource-base, and by the human resources which would flow from this. (Of course it is crucial that this should be an addition to 'social expenditures', and not, as the Lottery has become, a regressive alternative to taxation.) We might expect that many companies would commit expertise and skills to ensuring that 'their' resources were expended in ways creditable to them. We could hope to see a burgeoning of value-oriented activity, giving priority to goals and projects other than enrichment and consumption as such. This would be a way of replacing the generosity of investment in cultural and community goods that took place in medieval and early modern cities through churches and mosques, by secular agencies.

A number of sectors of public provision, including schools and residential care, could be fields in which 'voluntary sector' providers could take over a significant part of provision. Should it be possible for a non-profit association to set up a neighbourhood school, and bid for funding for it? Should we not value the diversity that would result from a larger number of social providers?

---

12. The CAF reports that British companies donate about £270 million per year to charities, of which £195 million comes from the top 500 companies. A one per cent contribution from all companies would increase this amount five-fold.

Already the cultural sector - theatres, arts centres and the like, much of community-based sport, and much environmental protection activity - substantially depends on this 'third economy' of subscriptions, grants, and frankly self-sacrificing work by individuals for the satisfaction of the work itself, and the social recognition that comes from doing it.

We might expect that such a development would win public support. The idea that corporations, and their shareholders, have some social obligation (extending to between one and five per cent of their pre-tax profits) would be likely to be widely accepted. The corporate sector is not as popular as the government seems to imagine. Many citizens are already involved in voluntary and community activities of some kind, and might be expected to identify with measures which give more support to these. The idea that more work would become available, of a kind which individuals could choose, would also be popular. The development of this sector offers an opportunity to widen the social alliance which supports New Labour, and feels identified with its achievements. The latent idealism expressed in the rejection of the Conservatives needs to be given some tangible expression.

There is, as Claus Offe has pointed out, a contradiction between the 'norm' of capitalist society, which enjoins and requires full-time paid work both to meet identity-needs and to earn the right to participate in the consumer culture, and its reality, which is of ever more citizens displaced from the labour market under one definition or another. The commodities which citizens wish to buy need a declining number of workers to produce them.

Some resolution of this dilemma should be sought in the expansion of a 'social' sector, distinct from the market or the state. We might hope that individuals would devote a proportion of their working lives to this sector, through intrinsic satisfaction and commitment, and for social and material recognition. There is especially a problem now that the state seems unlikely itself to take responsibility of employer of last resort.

In fact, relationships of family and friendship already have this intrinsic character. Stein Ringen in an interesting Demos pamphlet argued that one reason why higher standards of living have not generated a greater sense of well-being in America in recent years is because employees (especially women) have been forced to withdraw time and commitment from family and personal life in order to maintain their family earnings. If everyone works all the time for money, there is no time to have meals, conversations, to play, or go out together. Or to devote time to children, or aged parents.[13]

Two theme issues of Soundings - *The Public Good* (No 4) and *Active Welfare* (No 8) - have previously touched on these questions. The arguments of the current theme ruminate on the very different element of 'the personal' which is necessarily involved in many forms of labour. Several articles describe forms of work which are not motivated and organised just by bureaucratic edict nor by market incentive, but involve people joined together by values, beliefs, and a shared relation to task. Of course, in reality, such motivations and relationships inspire work in the private and state sectors, as well as those activities which are formally voluntary.[14] The voluntary sector has its own modes of compulsion and sometimes of exploitation. But still, the balances of motivation are often different between these spheres.

Those who choose to work in occupations felt to be most intrinsically satisfying (as actors, dancers, musicians, for example) already pay a premium, in lower incomes and less security, than if they chose their employment solely on material grounds. The same is true of other work involving a large element of social service - nursing and teaching, for example. The enlargement of the social sector, and the development of a larger national income stream to support it, would generate more work of intrinsically fulfilling kinds, providing an alternative to alienated but profitable employment on the one hand, and exclusion and isolation on the other.

Three sectors, not two

Social democracy has traditionally supported the existence of two major sectors, the public and the private, and has sought to establish some balance between

---

13. Stein Ringen, in his pamphlet *The Family in Question* (Demos 1998), points out that a huge proportion of national wealth is in reality generated by labour undertaken within households. He argues that our material standard of living would be less than half of what it is now if it were not for family production and co-operation. A question is how far such voluntary modes of co-operation can be extended outside the household.
14. Henry Neuburger, in an intervention in a *Soundings* discussion made a few weeks before he died suddenly in December, pointed out that the public sector, for example in the NHS or in schools, is to a great degree sustained by intrinsic loyalty and commitment. He argued that it is wrong to polarise the state as coercive, and the voluntary sector as altruistic in character. This valid observation suggests that how the public sector is organised is as crucial a question as how large it is.

them. This had relevance to employment as well as the balance of public and private services. The public sector offered greater security, and greater social protection, to its employees, at the cost of lower average wage and salary levels.

Our argument, which if implemented might give the Third Way some teeth, is for the recognition of three sectors, not two - a market, a state, and a dynamic non-profit sector. A social sector expanded by a contribution from corporate profits would need new forms of legal regulation, systems for allocating increase resources, and dedicated forms of education and training. There would need to be reflection on the likely consequences, both intended and unintended, of such a development, to make it work. Demos has taken considerable interest in this third sector, in its pamphlets on civic entrepreneurs and social entrepreneurs. However, the social sector from New Labour's point of view has been seen primarily as an alternative to the state, not equally as an alternative to business. The 'individualism' of the emphasis on the social entrepreneur reveals that what is envisaged is not so much new forms of social agency as a transfer of the qualities of business initiative to public services which are deemed to be bureaucratic and moribund.

Advocates of the 'Third Way' argue that new environments require new politics. More substance could be given to these ideas, by arguing that as well as the traditional social democratic countervailing powers to capitalism, there is scope for new kinds of counterbalance.

MR

'The individual is a minority'[1]

The thin line between universalism and particularism

Andreas Hess

Andreas Hess looks at current American debates on the relationship between the individual and society.

The reason that contemporary American debates on multiculturalism are receiving so much attention has much to do with the focus of the media on charismatic black leadership in the political, educational and cultural spheres. In promoting nationalism and open ethnocentrism - in short, particularism - charismatic figures such as Louis Farrakhan, Leonard Jeffries and Chuck D (to name just a few popular exponents who have surfaced in recent times) share a common objective: to give due attention to the social situation black Americans live in. It is argued that now political and civil rights have been achieved, it is time to fight for the social rights of black Americans - thereby assuring the identity of the black community. Yet whilst in the 1960s activists from diverse ethnic backgrounds fought together for the common goal of civil rights, the situation in the 1990s is quite different in that the particularistic trend has

---

1. Ralph Ellison, interview (1955), reprinted in Maryemma Graham and Amritjit Singh (eds), *Conversations with Ralph Ellison*, University of Mississippi Press, Jackson Mississippi 1995, p9.

become more prominent. To be sure, in the past the discourse within the black community had always bounced back and forth between particularistic and universalistic means and ends.[2] Yet the present situation is considerably different - both sociologically and politically. Firstly, the black community is no longer the largest minority group in the US but simply another minority among the many in a multicultural society. Secondly, the black community in itself has become differentiated - compared to people of other ethnic backgrounds, the spectrum of what black people can do and achieve is considerably broader than in the past - but, further than that, black America is internally more differentiated than ever before. It is my hypothesis that both factors - 'inward' and 'outward' differentiation, lie at the very heart of the current political debates on identity: black Americans have to come to terms with their identity, or better still their non-identity, in a changing environment. Having said that, one has to bear in mind that in a highly differentiated structure 'fine distinctions' (Pierre Bourdieu) can at once become major sources of conflict. In the face of both the 'inward' and 'outward' differentiation processes of the black community, individuals are challenged - and suddenly, defending or claiming group rights becomes a 'necessity' for determining one's individual identity.

The basic premise of my argument, as follows, is that the 'particularistic' discourse of Louis Farrakhan, Leonard Jeffries and various rappers does not in fact provide an appropriate answer to the complicated differentiation process, and neither do they provide the appropriate answer for the search for identity that results from such a differentiation process. Quite the opposite is true: even if we take unintended consequences into account, it is highly unlikely that universalistic ends will be achieved - that is a just society and, within it, individual fulfilment - through using particularistic means, for example, group rights. It is rather through the use of universalistic means, an approach which takes all individuals, independent of their race or ethnic origin, into account, that universalistic ends may be achieved - the universalistic ends of the well being and happiness of all individuals in a just society. There is, however, no firm guarantee for such a fortuitous outcome.

In what follows I would like to demonstrate that within the African-American

---

2. The debates between W.E.B. Du Bois and Booker T. Washington and Martin Luther King and Malcolm X are legendary in this respect.

intellectual discourse there have been and there are still voices that address the problem of identity/non-identity from a 'universalistic' standpoint - whilst at the same time not forgetting their 'particularistic' roots. In this respect I would cite the writer Ralph Ellison, before mentioning the literary critic Henry Louis Gates and the social philosopher Anthony Appiah as his successors. I would say that all three - Ellison, Gates and Appiah - provide an answer to the question of what identity or non-identity means to the black community - in direct opposition to the current obsession with and use of particularistic 'concepts' like nationalism and ethnocentrism. Additionally, I will briefly outline a conceptual framework for a new universalism: a universalism that takes difference into account. It is in this respect that I will refer firstly to Richard Rorty's notion of the individualist strand in leftist American social and political thought, before moving on to Jeffrey C. Alexander's conceptualisation of civil society.

Ralph Ellison

Many people may be familiar with Ralph Ellison, as the author of *Invisible Man*, but very few are familiar with Ralph Ellison the essay-writer, commentator, and critic of contemporary American culture. In various essays and interviews Ellison repeatedly challenged the view of colleagues and critics who see the individual author and all individuals solely as representatives of a certain social, in this case, a black background.

In a famous essay entitled 'The World and the Jug'[3] Ralph Ellison responded to an article by the New York critic Irving Howe on contemporary black literature.[4] Ellison starts by asking why it is that

> ... when critics confront the American as *Negro* they suddenly drop their advanced critical armament and revert with an air of confident superiority to quite primitive modes of analysis? Why is it that sociology-oriented critics seem to rate literature so far below politics and ideology that they would rather kill a novel than modify their presumptions concerning a given reality

---

3. First published in 1964, the essay was reprinted in *The Collected Essays of Ralph Ellison*, Saul Bellow (ed), The Modern Library, New York 1995.
4. Irving Howe, 'Black Boys and Native Sons' in *Dissent*, Autumn 1963.

which it seeks on its own terms to project. Finally, why is it that so many of those who would tell us the meaning of Negro life never bother to learn how varied it really is? (p155)

To be sure, these questions are not only directed and linked to aesthetics and literature. They go to the very heart of the white projection and white perception of how black people ought to live and write. Ellison strenuously challenges Howe's view that treats people of black origin not as individuals but rather as representatives of their ethnic background - thus denying any real individuality and subjectivity. Now one might well argue that, because of the peculiar history of slavery and the historical racist treatment of blacks in America, the factor of race does, to this day, matter greatly to the individual. Yet, as Ellison would argue, such a view does not challenge the role of the former victim; instead it reinforces and prolongs prejudice because the individual is still not considered as free and as having a 'proper' individuality. Ellison thus challenges a view of culture in which culture is seen solely as stemming from oppression and is therefore necessarily segregated. For Ellison, '...whatever the efficiency of segregation as a socio-political arrangement [was], it has been far from absolute on the level of culture' (p163). Here Ellison enters a new realm, a realm where culture is not limited to ethnicity or race, but rather becomes a common inheritance for all. In Ellison's words: 'Southern whites [and, I would add, in parenthesis, all other Americans independent of their race and ethnic origin] cannot walk, talk, sing, conceive of laws or justice, think of sex, love, the family or freedom without responding to the presence of Negroes' (p163). And against all common perceptions - including that of Irving Howe - Ralph Ellison insists that: '... it is not skin color which makes a Negro American but cultural heritage as shaped by the American experience, the social and political predicament, a sharing of that "concord of sensibilities" which the group expresses through historical circumstance and through which it has come to constitute a subdivision of the larger American culture' (p177). The individual is thus first an American and secondly a person with a particular (black) history. Having said this, it is also clear that the two stand in a dialectical relationship: all American history is part of black history and all black history is part of American history. There is thus a common inheritance on both sides and neither one can exist without the other. Ellison even goes a step further by saying that, if it is true that individuals have both sides in them, it is the individual that is subject to criticism - not the individual as a representative of a certain social group. In his answer to Irving Howe, Ellison suggests that he should

> ... ask himself in what way a Negro writer will achieve personal realisation (as a writer) *after* his people shall have won their full freedom. The answer appears to be the same in both instances: he will have to do it alone! He must suffer alone even as he shares the suffering of his group, and he must write alone and pit his talents against the standards set by the best practitioners of the craft, both past and present, in any case. For the writer's real way of sharing the experience of his group is to convert its mutual suffering into lasting value (p184).

It is quite clear that Ralph Ellison knows of no 'black culture' as defined by black nationalists. Ellison, as a commentary on his article in *The Atlantic* noted, was not the most popular person among radicals because he 'challenges the defence mechanisms of the black community'. He further challenges 'the underlying assumption of black radicals ... that whites have a monopoly on individuality and intelligence and, in order for a black man to lay claim to his own, he must necessarily change colour'. [5] In contrast to such particularistic talk, Ellison's objective is to claim back individuality and humanism without neglecting one's origins. He states:

> ... what we need is individuals. If the white society has tried to do anything to us, it has tried to keep us from being individuals. There's no reason why the individual can't be a member of a group. And, incidentally, the people who make the greatest cry against individuals are themselves trying to be the leaders. You can't miss *this* irony. They're doing all they can to suppress all individuality except their Own. This is *nonsense*. This we do not need. We need as many individuals developing their individual talents as possible, *but* dedicating some part of their energies to the experience of the group (*Indivisible Man*, p393).

---

5. Ralph Ellison and James Alan McPherson, 'Indivisible Man' (1970), reprinted in *The Collected Essays of Ralph Ellison*, p356, 395, see note 3.1 Ibid., p 393f.

It is almost unnecessary to say that Ellison's view does not only apply to writers but to all individuals in search of their identity. The writer, in Ellison's view, stands out in particular only because his or her case displays the most developed self-reflexive form of individuality.

Henry Louis Gates and Anthony Appiah

'"Race" as a meaningful criterion within the biological sciences has long been recognised to be a fiction ... Nevertheless, our conversations are replete with usages of *race* which have their sources in the dubious pseudo-science of the eighteenth and nineteenth centuries,' observes Henry Louis Gates.[6] Gates does not stop with this critical remark; he actually offers an explanation of why the obsession with race is still occupying America's mind. In his view 'race is the ultimate trope of difference because it is so very arbitrary in its application (*LC*, p49). In other words, differences that principally can be overcome are essentialised - essentialised in a way that makes differences appear to be 'fixed and finite categories' (Gates) - 'second nature' so to speak.

Any serious attempt that tries to come to terms with 'blackness' and the individual must overcome such an essentialist view. But how can this be done without falling into the trap of an abstract humanistic universalism - a universalism that does not take any cultural and social peculiarities into account? And how can this be done without reaching the other extreme, of substituting 'white essentialism' with 'Blackness' - which fundamentally represents another essentialism? According to Gates one can only overcome the essentialist or abstract universalistic view by taking race as '... a text (an array of discursive practices), not an essence' (*LC*, p79). Gates argues in the spirit of Ralph Ellison when he rages against what he calls 'our own version of the Thought Police, who would determine who, and what, is "black"' (*LC*, p127). He argues for the United States as being a multicoloured country where 'blackness without blood' is 'what we must pass on' (*LC*, p127). But how can this be advanced categorically? To provide an answer, Gates looks at the 'holy male trinity' consisting of Richard Wright, James Baldwin and Ralph Ellison. While Wright is perceived of as following the enlightenment tradition,

---

6. In *Loose Canons. Notes on Cultural Wars* (Hereafter *LC*), Oxford University Press, New York 1992, p48.

since it is this tradition that is colour blind (in Gates's view, Wright never tried to take a closer look at himself), blackness for James Baldwin becomes a salvation for both white and black America. A much more sophisticated answer came from Ralph Ellison. For him, 'blackness was a metaphor of the human condition ... yet ... (achieved) through a faithful adherence to its particularity' (LC, p142). In Gates's view it is exactly Ellison's Hegelian notion of the universal in the particular and vice versa that makes it possible to conceive of identity processes of individuals as being universalistically oriented in means and ends while at the same time acknowledging the particular history of an ethnic group. It is precisely this attitude which allows Gates to have it both ways: 'I want to be black, to know black, to luxuriate in whatever I might be calling blackness at any particular time - but to do so in order to come out the other side, to experience a humanity that is neither colorless nor reducible to color. Bach *and* James Brown. Sushi *and* fried catfish'.[7]

The social philosopher Anthony Appiah is quite close to Gates's views in his attempt to discuss the meaning of being 'colour conscious'.[8] Appiah argues against all attempts at dividing the human race into different races and related cultures. Rather he proposes differentiating between the analytical and the normative discourse of analysis. On the analytical level, Appiah suggests using a Sartrean approach - racism and its social consequences can indeed be phenomenologically observed - yet at the same time the observer must not confuse social cultural difference with biology (a view which usually stems from essentialising the social fact that individuals and groups are judged by other human beings and groups on the basis of the colour of their skin). For the analysis of historical discourses, Appiah's proposal would involve reflecting upon and investigating with a critical eye such terms as 'Africans', 'Negroes', 'Coloured People', 'Blacks', 'Afro-Americans' or 'African Americans'. It would not only mean writing the history of these signifiers, but also taking a closer look at their social and political implications and their possible effects.

Appiah warns of confusing the two levels of discourse: what seems to be acceptable on the analytical level is completely unacceptable on the

---

7. Henry Louis Gates, *Colored People*, Knopf, New York 1994, pxv.
8. Anthony Appiah and Amy Gutmann, *Color Conscious*, Princeton University Press, Princeton 1996.

normative level. He has no doubts that ethnic identity could become a forum for the purpose of confronting racism, yet he warns of making ethnic identity a new cause for future tyranny. Here, the social philosopher argues for making an intellectual effort: he aims at maintaining a balance between the meaning of difference, of what he calls 'human identity', on one side, and the fundamental moral unity which is valid for humanity as a whole on the other side. Anthony Appiah has thus elevated the discourse of identity and difference to a new level - a new level where it is possible to discuss identity (and/or even non-identity) and how it relates to difference, without forgetting the pace-setting normative values.[9]

Yet we should not forget that behind all intellectual statements lurk concrete social conditions, and behind all the talk about differences it is not difficult to identify larger drifts in and of modern society. Multicultural America can serve as a good example. The change of macro-sociological patterns - for example demographic shifts resulting from changing immigration patterns - has had an impact on the micro-level - from shifting patterns of interaction to identity-formation **'Bach *and* James Brown. Sushi *and* fried catfish'** processes of individuals. Thus when individual life styles become crucial, 'fine distinctions' can suddenly turn into major forces of identity formation processes. It has been hypothesised here that the re-emergence of the particularistic creed serves precisely this purpose of differentiating oneself from the social group one belongs to, and that which applies to daily life is necessarily repeated on the intellectual level as well. Thus much of the current rhetoric of multiple yet separate identities - most prominent in the field of 'cultural studies' - can be interpreted as a response to the differentiation process and internal stratification of modern society. Having said this, one must bear in mind that it is a false response; it simply reiterates and reinforces the 'Bennettonisation' (Gates) of society and culture on an intellectual level without breaking down the boundaries of biologically or culturally 'grounded' racist talk. According to Anthony Appiah it is the task of intellectuals to resist

9. If this is a way of squaring the circle when addressing the issue of difference - so be it! The public debate in the United States has already benefited from the rediscovery of universalism by the 'new black intellectuals': after the antisemitic remarks of Farrakhan and Jeffries, reconciliation must certainly be on the agenda.

such 'imperialism of identity'. But does the opposite of squaring the circle, the promotion of a new 'universal universalism' that takes difference into account, make sense and does it really provide an answer to the urgent questions outlined above? In order to answer this question, I would like to refer briefly to Richard Rorty's discussion on leftist thought in twentieth-century America, before finally highlighting the notions of civil society as outlined by Jeffrey C. Alexander.

The individual and civil society

In *Achieving Our Country*, Richard Rorty discusses the contemporary state the American political left is in.[10] This discussion is directly relevant to our problem since Rorty takes on what he calls the 'Foucauldian', 'cultural left'. According to Rorty, the cultural left is obsessed with 'otherness', 'ineradicable stigma' and the 'ubiquity of power' - hence it is only logical that 'Satan' and 'original sin' are the 'problems' the Foucauldian left is preoccupied with. (Of course Rorty is speaking metaphorically. 'Satan' refers to the all-powerful social system, while 'original sin' refers to the fact that the social system seems to be so prevalent, that to be part of it means exercising some of its structural power - regardless of individual positions or views.) The use of metaphysical metaphors suggests that Rorty regards the theoretical efforts from which the cultural left derives its concepts as the secularised equivalent to religion. What Rorty wants to stress here is that there is nothing in the American leftist perception of Lacan's 'impossible objects of desire', Derrida's notion of 'differential subjectivity', or Foucault's notion of power, which suggests that there could be such a thing as a political agent. (As a matter of fact, according to the criticised line of reasoning, it does not even make sense to talk about individuals and individuality any more.) As power becomes structural, it also becomes invisible - in short, metaphysical. Politically, Rorty considers this to be a disaster. If difference and otherness are preserved and perpetuated as counterweights to the structural powers that be, there can no longer be a sense of common ground - apart, perhaps, from the sum of all differences. (It would indeed be deeply

---

10. Richard Rorty, *Achieving Our Country - Leftist Thought in Twentieth-Century America*, Harvard University Press, Cambridge Massachusetts 1998.

enshrined in the logic of the sum of all differences to be unable to pursue a common cause; not even laws could be proposed from such a standpoint - since it is the essence of laws to abstract from all differences in order to make them applicable to all individuals.) It is such internal contradictions of 'the politics of difference' that lead Rorty to the verdict that if such a path were pursued further, deliberative leftist politics would cease to exist.

Rorty promotes a radical paradigm change: if there is to be a successful American left in the future, it will have to see people no longer as mere spectators and victims, but rather as agents pursuing individual goals - and it will be only through individual achievement that difference will be respected and treated accordingly.[11] But how can such a state of individual achievement and difference be reached? Rorty stresses that maintaining difference for its own sake makes little sense. Logically then, for him, the 'romance of endless diversity' not 'multiculturalism' is the solution. Multiculturalism only 'suggests a morality of live-and-let-live, a politics of side-by-side development in which members of distinct cultures preserve and protect their own culture against the incursions of other cultures' (AOC, p24). In opposition to such a viewpoint, Rorty suggests pursuing the Hegelian project of the struggle for acceptance - i.e. competition, arguments and discussion between members of various cultures - in order to achieve a synthesis, a new and better culture, consisting of a 'variety in unity'. Furthermore, Rorty stresses that the solution can only be a political one, based on shared and reliable democratic institutions and citizenship.[12]

However, in Rorty's account, the social realm remains somehow void. He might be a good philosopher and a decent political theorist, yet he has little to say about the social and societal conditions under which such conceived individualism and difference could compete and indeed flourish. There is for example nothing in Rorty's account that explains why it is that

---

11. It was Marx who thought that the achievement of individual happiness should always be the objective. In one of the most misquoted sentences of the Communist Manifesto he writes: 'We shall have an association in which the free development of each is the condition for the free development of all'.
12. This seems to me to be *the* major contradiction in Rorty: he supports the idea of citizenship, yet he abhors everything that reminds him of universalism or universal values.

we are now witnessing the numerous discussions about the possible contradictions between political and social, individual and group rights. Rorty can certainly provide answers when it comes to the normative implications, but he is at odds when discussing the real social dimensions of individual competition and difference. In particular he seems to have absolutely no clear notion of how differentiated and complex modern society can be; furthermore, he has no notion of any of the universalistic dimensions that lie behind citizenship.

In response to Rorty's intellectual void, I hypothesise here that it is only through the conceptual framework of Jeffrey C. Alexander - particularly his conceptualisation of modern, differentiated civil society - that we begin to understand the complicated sociological side of the argument on difference. In order to acknowledge the depth of Alexander's point of view, we must take a brief look at intellectual history. Alexander distinguishes between three different forms of civil society. Civil society I was first conceptualised by such thinkers as Ferguson and Smith, Rousseau, Hegel and Tocqueville, and referred to an early umbrella-like broad variety of institutions outside the state: i.e. religious groups, private and public organisations, public opinion and institutions. In contrast, civil society II stands not for a further elaboration of the idea as one would expect, but rather for a narrowed-down version of the original concept in that civil society becomes associated solely with market capitalism. Political equality and rights, in short, citizenship, are denounced as being only formally equal. Instead of political equality, Marx in particular preferred to promote substantive social equality. It is indeed a cunning move within history that it proved to be the right that interpreted and perpetuated this logic, in that they attempted to abolish all social controls in order to give more space to the market. The left was no better in that they thought it appropriate to abolish the market all together - either practically, as was witnessed in the communist countries, or theoretically as displayed in much of Western Marxist thought. Yet, as we approach the end of the century, we are witness to the emergence of civil society III - a society in which differentiation leads to a social realm that can be explained neither by referring to the state nor to the capitalist market on their own. Alexander describes this social realm as '... a solidarity sphere in which a certain kind of universalising community comes gradually to be defined and to some degree enforced.'[13] He further explains: 'To the degree this solidary community exists, it is exhibited by "public opinion", possesses its own cultural codes and narratives in a democratic idiom, is patterned by a set of peculiar institutions, most notably legal and journalistic ones, and is visible in historically distinctive sets of international practices like civility, equality, criticism, and respect.' He adds finally: 'This kind of civil community can never exist as such; it can only "to one degree or another". One reason is that it is always interconnected with, and interpenetrated by, other, more and less differentiated spheres which have their own criteria of justice and their own system of rewards. There is no reason to privilege any one of these non-civil spheres over any other.'

These quotes can be read as an abstract of Alexander's attempts at conceptualising the differentiation within modern society. The development of different social spheres, each with its own relative autonomy that is irreducible to other spheres (and also the communication between the different spheres) seems to be central to an understanding of how modern civil society functions. It also becomes clear that to select one discourse above another is not to conceptualise late twentieth century civil society in terms of nineteenth-century developments and, more crucially, it also means giving in to the uncivil dimensions of civil society. Whether socialists argue the need to get rid of civil society because it is utterly bourgeois, or radical feminists argue that civil society is inherently patriarchal, or black nationalists think of racism as a natural part of civil society - all these discourses suffer from the generalisation of particular discourses and deny the complexity of modern civil society. Furthermore, as Alexander stresses, these highly selective uncivil discourses are deeply anti-individualist in that they reject the unique history of individualism in Western societies - particularly the contributions to modern civil society of Christianity, the Renaissance, the Reformation, the Enlightenment and Romanticism.

To sum up, Alexander's conception of civil society not only allows us to be critical of the anti-individualist discourse of the Foucauldian left; its further advantage is that it also allows us to conceptualise the uncivil dimensions of civil society and to conceive thus of possible answers to the challenge posed.

---

13. Jeffrey C. Alexander, *Real Civil Societies*, Sage, London 1998, pp1-19. This quote and the next two can be found on p7.

Having begun this piece with the literary intervention of Ralph Ellison and the new black intellectuals and having ended with Richard Rorty's emphasis on competitive individuality and Alexander's notion of modern civil society, we have gone full circle: what first appeared to be a passionate defence of individual achievement in literature and culture on the side of the new black intellectuals, and such leftist intellectuals as Richard Rorty, develops into a serious analysis of differentiated American society, and a defence of the achievements of modern American democracy - at least in terms of its universalist notions of citizenship. After what has been said, my final point of reference to C.L.R. James should not now be completely unexpected. It was indeed C.L.R. James who held on to both universalist and individualist values. He rejected all particularistic concepts that were not linked to notions of the universal - in terms of both means and ends. When invited to comment on a new Black Studies programme in Washington, James said, 'to talk to me about black studies as if it's something that concerned black people is an utter denial. This is the history of Western Civilisation. I can't see it otherwise. This is the history that black people and white people and all serious students of modern history and the history of the world have to know. To say it's some kind of ethnic problem is a lot of nonsense.'[14]

---

14. C.L.R. James, Anna Grimshaw (ed), *The C.L.R. James Reader*, Blackwell, Oxford 1992, p397.

Five poems

Harbour

On the pier that morning
I waited for you
in my tailored coat
and sheepskin gloves.
I was first up
leaving early before breakfast.
There was no-one else
only a man delivering milk and pies
fishing boats pulled up on the shore
and the stone church
stunned with cold.

Frances Angela

Sister

What I feel for you is not love exactly
but I would like to hear from you again,

your voice hooting from a distance
like those trains across the Far Field

in that hard place where we found ourselves,
where we passed in the corridors without speaking

and were not allowed to sit together. The conversation
at meals prepared us for what we must expect.

We learned to be cold and stiff. To observe distance.
Outside the cold swing hung in its chains

the flannels froze overnight as we slept
in our separate houses under those strict blankets.

You said I could go home if I was not happy
which was not true. What I felt was not love

exactly. I thought you might take my hand
and lead me down Driffield Terrace to the station.

I know now you could not have learned
that kind of behaviour in that kind of place.

We have changed our names. Only by chance
would we come together now on any list, in any order.

Dorothy Nimmo

The Manifesto

That mound of cloth, not there before we left,
Grown like a fungus from the African earth,
Speaks through a stick once green upon a tree
Now scathed white by age and use.
This creature with hidden head,
No legs to walk
Or voice to talk,
With two black fingers poking through the rags
Rolls the stick slowly forwards through the dust,
Bone upon wood, wood upon earth,
Declaring that as the stick had been a tree,
He had been a man.

Michael Young

Letter to Grandad: Far from Home

In a garden
as yet unplanted with signs,
generations of memories,
once uprooted, warred by words,
now blossom into a single alphabet.
Letter by letter
we trace the news of peace:
'Shalom' telegraphed by wild mimosa
scenting barbed wire in every camp;
'Salaam' headlined in asphodel
amongst the ruined mosques.

We visit these histories
like tourists of the Unheimlich,
eyes straining for the foreign
in what is nearest home.
But why admire the living
only because they are not yet dead?
I search the family album
for snapshots of the future
where remembrance might become
other than resemblance
to the deja vu.

Failing better than usual
to find your last resting place
I stumble on these clues.

Phil Cohen

Wool Over My Eyes

When I think of the beginning, I remember
Rosy Catchpole knitting everywhere: summers,
in the playground; round the coke stove

in winter. Rib. Cable. Moss. She could pass
slipped stitches over whole jumpers
while we were still unpicking dishcloths.

A round shouldered old woman at ten,
with eyebrows which sloped like a circumflex
in perpetual perplexity at everything,

she didn't care if she failed the 11+ -
the Grammar was a bus-ride too far for her.
I can see her, agog while I bragged

about where I was going, lording it
with stories of midnight feasts swallowed
from my sister who was full of it.

Rosy Catchpole. The sudden cessation
of the click, click, ominous as a clock
stopping. Her shocked: "Oh! I couldn't.
I'd miss my mum." And the penny dropping.

Frances Wilson

Storming the Millennium
The New Politics of Change
Edited by Tim Jordan and Adam Lent

Recommended retail price £12.99.
Available to *Soundings* readers for
£10.99 post free.

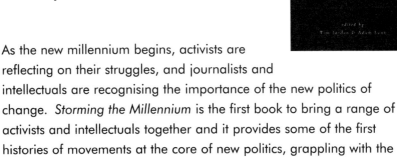

As the new millennium begins, activists are reflecting on their struggles, and journalists and intellectuals are recognising the importance of the new politics of change. *Storming the Millennium* is the first book to bring a range of activists and intellectuals together and it provides some of the first histories of movements at the core of new politics, grappling with the important political and theoretical issues they raise.

Bringing together new and established writers, *Storming the Millennium* includes discussions of crime and justice, disabilities, bisexual, gay, lesbian and transgender politics, race issues in 1990s Britain and activism on the Internet. It also addresses the relationship between new politics, the new left and socialism.

Contributors: Peter Beresford, Tessa Bird, Patrick Field, Tony Fitzpatrick, Nancy Fraser, Stuart Hall, Shirin Housee, Rupa Huq, Tim Jordan, Adam Lent, Doreen Massey, Michael Rustin, Sanjay Sharma, Merl Storr.

Please send cheque for £10.99 made out to Lawrence and Wishart to L&W, 99a Wallis Road London E9 5LN.

English Imaginaries
Anglo-British Approaches
to Modernity
Kevin Davey

Recommended retail price £12.99.
Available to Soundings readers for
£10.99 post free.

What does it mean to be English in the modern world? The answer doesn't usually include Nancy Cunard's assault on Anglo British whitenes, J. B. Priestley's democratic populism, Who guitarist Pete Townshend's modernist rebellion, Vivienne Westwood's anti-fashion, David Dabydeen's blackening of the literary and visual canon or Mark Wallinger's detourement of English oil painting. Kevin Davey, drawing on the work of Gramsci and Julia Kristeva, argues that it should and goes on to ask some searching questions about New Labour's vision of the nation.

> 'With this book the debate about Englishness grows up. In his profound meditation Kevin Davey puts to shame most of the recent spate of essays on this fashionable theme.' Anthony Barnett

South Asia

Fifty years after independence

T.V. Sathyamurthy

Against the background of globalisation, T. V. Sathyamurthy assesses political and economic developments in South Asia since independence, and argues that fundamental change can best be achieved by building a participatory democracy.

As we approach the new century, we are witnessing changes of far-reaching political significance at all levels: global, international, regional, national and local. One of these changes is the important transition that is under way in South Asia.

The region as a whole has experienced five decades of governance through structures of power bequeathed by European colonial rulers. And despite its apparent resilience and undoubted puissance, the state (and those who control its power) in South Asia has shown a marked reluctance to encourage the development of democratic political practice and people's participation in the determination of the thrust of governmental policy.

During the last twenty years, the structures of power in South Asia have been challenged by movements of resistance which have raised demands to secure the elementary (democratic, civil and human) rights of poor and socially oppressed peoples. With the onset of globalisation, and its consequences for the social polarisation and economic differentiation of the better-off middle classes and the impoverished masses, struggles have multiplied to create political spaces in the body politic conducive to democratic practice.

The literature that has accumulated under the social science disciplinary rubrics of International Relations and Development has been silent on matters relating to democratic practice (as distinct from formal democracy) in Asia. It is based on the assumption that those parts of the world where post-colonial structures (recognisably similar to those of the metropolitan powers) prevail are democratic, and those that are ideologically divergent from the Western democracies are undemocratic. The possibility that the former might, in actuality, turn out to be essentially undemocratic or unequal or both, and that the latter might have, hidden in their interstices, oases of democratic practice is seldom given serious consideration in social science writings on the dynamics of democratic politics.

This essay attempts to provide an analysis of the present juncture in South Asian politics from a perspective of international relations and development. The importance of the international dimension should be obvious. With the disappearance of the Soviet Union, followed by the transformation of the world (at least for the time being) into a One-Superpower-Dominant international system, a qualitative change has occurred in the post-cold war re-configurations of power. The virtual disappearance of two of the three major contradictions of the cold war era, and the retreat to the back burner of the third, has provided a massive stimulus to the processes of globalisation, marketisation, liberalisation, privatisation, modernisation and de-regulation.[1] The poorer parts of the world, South Asia among them, have been disproportionately affected by this development. With the demise of planning and the shrinkage of the public sector, poverty has greatly increased during the last fifteen years, in an already poor, highly differentiated and unevenly developing (and underdeveloping) economy.

Changes in Asia and the world

In the re-configuration of political forces in the aftermath of the cold war, we must not lose sight of realignments among the three great established economic powers: the USA, Europe (meaning the European Union or EU) and Japan. Of

---

1. I have discussed these elsewhere. In short, the major contradictions of the cold war period can be characterised as those between (1) the two superpowers and their allies; (2) the two major communist countries and their allies; and (3) the forces of national liberation and the forces of imperialism.

these, Japan is both a modern economic power and an Asian country with a powerful stake in the ongoing economic, political and strategic transformations of that continent. These realignments of potential sources of agglomerations of economic power will, in all likelihood, give rise to contradictions within the giant power configuration made up of these three areas of the world. Moreover, the radical changes under way are fuelled by new ramifications of capital in a world of thinning if not shrinking national boundaries, and increasing fiscal porosity; and they are accompanied by the almost evangelical zeal with which latter day converts to capitalism and to newly-opened areas of capitalist penetration foster the expansion of markets.

During the next twenty years, China (with the integration of Hong Kong followed by Macao and, eventually, Taiwan) will almost certainly experience an exponential surge in its economic performance. Such a development is bound to give rise to new stresses affecting China's economic and political relations with the rest of Asia, as well as with the Western world in general and the USA in particular. The major contradiction of the world during the first half of the twenty-first century may well crystallise around the project of the modernisation and globalisation of the Chinese economy. As has been the case in Japan during the second half of this century, so too in China during the next fifty years, a continued low-profile projection of itself in the military sphere is likely to be more than offset by a spectacular economic performance in line with its newly embraced faith in capitalism.

From a perspective of development, South Asia constitutes a significant area of the Asian continent, which is of strategic interest to the global powers including Japan and a rising China. It is also one of the three major regions of the Asian continent, the others being the Far East (including North-East Asia) and South-East Asia. Despite sharing some similarities, these three regions are remarkably divergent in their economic, political and social characteristics, and in their underlying dynamics.

In a global context of power, the three large Asian states of Japan, China and India offer contrasts that are germane to future trends in international relations. Japan is an economic superpower exercising an influence that rivals America's. With the anti-imperialist national liberation struggles thrown out of gear since the 1980s, it would appear on the surface that the path of capitalist development has been cleared of major obstacles to the processes of globalisation and liberalisation. But it would be unwise to jump to the conclusion that such a development would automatically act as an indefinite guarantee of USA hegemony over any part of Asia. For the determination of China to become a full-fledged member of the capitalist club, and the likely emergence of India as an unevenly but substantially developed though dependent capitalist economy, may have far from palatable consequences for America.

One of the implications of the development of China and India at the present rate is that they will compete in a major way with the older European powers and America for access to raw materials. At the same time, such a development of China and India will almost certainly result in a rapid expansion of the world's middle classes (on an upward consumption curve, of course), by an order of magnitude of another billion in the next two decades or so, and they will thus outnumber by a substantial margin the bourgeois population of the rest of the world.

The crisis of 'sustainability', not to mention global pollution levels, will reach proportions hitherto undreamed of. The West in general, and the USA in particular, will have to devise new strategies, including a possible, arguably voluntary, lowering of the consumption pattern of their own middle classes, or face the alternative of conflict with the new Asian members of the global capitalist club. Paradoxically, the dialectic of the post-cold war era of 'doors opening' in third areas of the world may well give rise to consequences not dissimilar to those feared during the era of national liberation struggles.[2] The rise of new poles of growth within a globalised capitalist system will in all likelihood lead to a clash between its established dominant and newly emergent segments.

Let us now move south, in the Asian context, for the purposes of this discussion. The emerging picture can be completed with a brief reference to the formation of regional identities in South-East Asia and South Asia. We have already noted that in north and east Asia, two major economic forces are on the threshold of radical change. Japan is undergoing a process of re-adjustment of its post-war role as a Western economic power of global significance. At the same time, as a more and more vigorous member of an emergent cohort of Asian economic giants, it is establishing powerful links with

---

2. Especially as prefigured in the indiscriminate use of the domino metaphor.

China, South-East Asia and (to a lesser extent) South Asia.

Despite its relatively uneven development, China enjoys the advantages that go with its continental size. Japan's great opportunity lay in its Phoenix-like rise from the ashes of Armageddon to become one of the economic super-powers of the century. Unlike either China or Japan, until the 1960s the ASEAN (Association of South East Asian Nations) members were embroiled in internal and regional struggles that stood in the way of rapid economic development. The region as a whole became a theatre of tension between nationalist, pro-American and pro-communist political forces. However, the entire region was somewhat less susceptible to uneven development than South Asia or even China, though it started from a low threshold of industrialisation and modernisation.

During the last three decades, the different parts of the region - from the vast archipelago of Indonesia to relatively small nations - have come together to forge close institutional links, and programmes of mutual Cupertino and division of labour, in the spheres of investment, production and export. In the process, they have learnt the art of promoting their collective or regional identity without allowing themselves to be held back by rigidly conceived ideas of national sovereignty. So much so that ASEAN, the crisis of 1997 notwithstanding, is second only to the EU in contemporary world politics in the quality and level of economic performance that it has achieved, through a combination of techniques and practices based on the principles of integration, complexity and subsidiarity.

As a region, South-East Asia is not in the same league as Japan or China (given the latter's potential). Nevertheless, it represents a tranche of Asian economic development of considerable magnitude and importance, continuing to rise on an upward curve. South-East Asia has thus carved out for itself a dynamic role, even allowing for the radical political changes that await some countries of the region (e.g. Indonesia) in the near future.

The problem of South Asia

In striking contrast to South East Asia, South Asian countries (mostly nations with a background of British colonial rule) have been stuck in a groove for far too long.[3] As a region, South Asia has not changed radically. Even recent injections of strong doses of modernisation and liberalisation, globalisation and

---

3. Afghanistan, Bangladesh, Bhutan, India, Maldives, Nepal, Pakistan and Sri Lanka.

marketisation, have not quite awakened South Asian nation states from their prolonged state of post-colonial torpor. There are several important characteristics which mark out the South Asian cohorts from their South-East Asian counterparts.

Firstly, South Asian countries have been unable to shed the legacy of inter-regional, inter-communal, inter-ethnic, and inter-religious tensions bequeathed by colonial rule. Far from diluting them and blazing new trails of mutual co-operation, the dominant classes in control of state structures in these countries have invariably sought to exploit the various tensions present in the society for political purposes. The subordination of social ends to sectional gain has been an enduring feature of intra-ruling class conflicts in different countries of the region.

Secondly, in the economic sphere, entrenched agrarian structures have proved difficult to reform. Even though the capitalist mode of production has penetrated agriculture, pre-capitalist relations of production as well as traditional social hierarchies have continued to flourish. The political consequences of this co-habitation, within the economic base, of two fundamentally opposed forces of production, have remained counter-productive to rapid economic growth.

At the same time, technological self-reliance has developed only partially even in India, which has claimed credit for a long-term policy of self-sufficiency and autochthonous development. The success of the forces of globalisation and modernisation throughout South Asia has been much less apparent than in South-East Asia, or, for that matter, in any other region of Asia. Uneven development in an era of central planning (1950s-1980s, especially in India and Sri Lanka) has reproduced itself under different conditions during the present epoch of modernisation (starting in the 1990s). As a consequence, the rate of economic growth in South Asia can be expected to fall drastically behind the rate of economic growth of South-East Asia.

A third salient difference lies in the fact that throughout the first five decades of the post-colonial history of the region, relations between South Asian countries have been fraught with conflict: over borders, over territorial and irredentist disputes, over ideological questions (e.g. secular democracy *versus* theocratic autocracy), over ethnic separatism and national fusion (e.g. Sri Lanka) and over questions relating to 'internal colonialism' (leading, for example, to the break-up of Pakistan and the establishment of Bangladesh, and, subsequently, to tensions between the Centre and/or Punjab on the one hand and sister provinces of Pakistan on the other). There has also been conflict in the aftermath of Soviet military intervention in Afghanistan and the civil strife which followed; and there is the predicament of the small land-locked kingdoms of Nepal and Bhutan with a big regional power breathing down their necks.

The arrogant behaviour of India towards other South Asian countries, its doomed China policy of the 1960s and 1970s, the intransigence of India and Pakistan over Kashmir, and India's uneven record on the Tamil question relating to Sri Lanka, have been among the serious obstacles blocking social and economic progress in the region as a whole.

'A lion's share of the responsibility for South Asia's miserable record in the maintenance of intra-regional peace thus belongs to India'

A lion's share of the responsibility for South Asia's miserable record in the maintenance of intra-regional peace thus belongs to India which, under the dominance of the Congress Party, tended to treat the region more as its fiefdom than as a community of equal, separate, independent states. Non-Congress coalitions (as well as the Congress government that was briefly presided over by Lal Bahadur Shastri), however, have pursued policies clearly accented towards tempering the inequalities of intercourse; but the Congress Party has not yet remained continuously out of power for a sufficient length of time to create conditions that would favour a breaking of the mould in which the international relations of South Asia have been set.

A fourth difference between South-East Asian societies and South Asia lies in their different post-colonial developmental experience. In South Asia, unlike in South-East Asia, not only has development been extremely uneven, it has also been accompanied by an intensification of poverty reflected in an acute downward differentiation along a vertical axis among all social strands; there has also been a systematic disempowerment of large segments of society; a drastic shrinkage of social opportunities; and massive deprivation caused by the lack of entitlement of a vast majority of the population to elementary civic democratic and social rights, to education, health and employment.

Thus, in India, to cite a ready example, a majority of the population has sunk to such depths of deprivation that they lie submerged beneath even the officially defined poverty line; by the same token, the Sri Lankan economy which, during the early years of independence, held promise of an adequate welfare policy, is plagued by poverty at levels comparable to that prevailing elsewhere in the region. Poverty in Bangladesh is experienced in rural areas through agricultural involution and in the towns through a grossly dependent, partially criminalised and stagnant urban economy. Long periods of military rule and endemic corruption of civilian political parties have also contributed to an intensification of poverty in countries such as Bangladesh and Pakistan.

The state and the economy

The state is by far the most puissant political actor in South Asian, as in East Asian and South-East Asian, countries. However, its social foundations differ radically between these regions. Starting from an advanced economic base, Japan rebuilt itself under post-war American occupation and a regime of 'liberal democratisation' of the civilian polity. China, under the CCP, rigorously pursued a dynamic policy during the 1949-79 period (preceded by a highly enlightened radical economic policy that belonged to the Yenan era) of eradicating poverty and enabling the lowest rungs of society to secure the basic entitlements - health, housing, literacy and education, employment, minimum welfare and democratic political participation at the local level (the term 'democratic' being radically differently understood in this context from the standard Western view). In South Korea and Taiwan, economic development was pursued with the help of huge amounts of money made available by the USA (an almost suzerain presence in both countries) as well as drastic land reform radically altering the productive agricultural base. In South-East Asian countries, despite a lack of clear commitment to the eradication of poverty, the new states (whether under the control of populist governments as in Indonesia under Sukarno's leadership or Malaysia under UMNO, or in the form of a civil-military hybrid as in Thailand or Indonesia since the 1965 overthrow of Sukarno) would appear to have built their economic edifices in social milieus that have been significantly less harsh than in South Asia.

In contrast to all the other regions of Asia, throughout South Asia the state has, on balance, played a negative role in relation to the economic position of the mass of the population, which has steadily worsened over the years. At the same time, state power has been generously deployed towards the creation of a substantial minority belonging to the middle class (numbering about 300 million in India, 50 million in Pakistan, 5 million in Sri Lanka, and 15 million in Bangladesh, with far fewer in Afghanistan, Nepal and Bhutan).

A comparative analysis of the structure of poverty in the different regions of Asia, and in different countries within each region, can throw light on the political pressure points that are developing in different societies in the domestic, regional and international contexts. Of particular relevance here is the question of the intensification of poverty and uneven development in China, recently opened to the outside world, against a background of three decades of successful struggle to remove mass deprivation within a 'closed system'.

However, the price of dependent and centralised development has been exacted in the form of an accelerating 'democratic deficit' (in electoral polities) or of outright 'authoritarianism' (in states that oscillate between absolutisms of one kind or another).

Unlike horizontal social contradictions (i.e. those occurring within a social stratum), which invariably lend themselves to intra-ruling class accommodation, vertical social contradictions (e.g. between the state and the mass of the people, between industrial capital and labour, between the rich and middle peasantry and the poor peasantry and landless labour, between men and women in the family and at the workplace) tend to intensify with development. A general factor underlying this phenomenon is the differentiation between the upwardly mobile better off and the downwardly mobile worse/worst off resulting in an exacerbation of poverty and deprivation.

Finally, seen from the grassroots, the structure of the state in South Asia (as indeed in other parts of Asia, to differing degrees) constitutes an alienating phenomenon. Even in countries, such as India, in which some form of token decentralisation (*panchayati raj*) of power has been reluctantly brought into being, local structures to which power has been devolved (with few exceptions) take no steps to spread the benefits of decentralised power to the population as a whole. A yawning gap separates the local 'haves', who monopolise the resources, and the mass of the local 'poor'. Environmental and ecological damage and abuse inflicted by development projects affect the latter, whilst the benefits flow to the former.

In all countries of South Asia, democratic consciousness and an awareness of civil rights has grown among the poorer sections. A minimal impact of this expanding sense of political identity can be seen in the alacrity and thoroughness with which the mass of the electorate periodically wipes the slate clean of legislators and parties with a manifestly corrupt record. However, the electoral astuteness of the mass of the people is by no means sufficient to change the agenda of the state or the commitment of the dominant classes to further their own class interests (with the assistance, needless to add, of their international mentors and supporters), rather than the common interests of all classes of society.

An enormous rift has developed during the last three decades between political parties whose horizon does not reach beyond the narrow confines of the classes that they represent and the vast and expanding mass of (undifferentiated) poor. This has led to a growing realisation that democratic ends cannot be vouchsafed by the existing modalities of state power and socio-economic development.

Thus we have been witnessing a growth of political and social movements addressing problems of an immediate nature, including how to survive under conditions of increasingly harsh and ruthless exploitation at the hands of the structures of the state and of the local power-holders, and how to safeguard the environment, and customarily available local resources for subsistence, from the depredations of 'developers'. In India, Sri Lanka, Bangladesh and Nepal, a vast number of local movements of resistance have registered remarkable though still limited successes, despite their continuing to remain parochially based and confined to single (or a small clutch of) issues. However, the important insight arising out of this observation is that democratic participation cannot be guaranteed simply by writing a constitution or by constructing instrumentalities of state.

The signal failure of the existing system of power in this area, during the last five decades, to acknowledge the need for giving political participation due importance, has resulted in the democratic initiative passing into the hands of the mass of the people (in the first instance, at the local level).

The state in South Asia is thus at a crossroads. To co-operate with their democratically aroused peoples or to resist them, that is the question. Resistance to an unheeding state has been the language of the poor in the face of opposition. How will the class forces that control the levers of state power respond to the new political consciousness that is spreading throughout the lower rungs of society?

I began this essay with a reference to contemporary developments in global inter-relationships. Briefly returning to the same theme, we can observe that the highly uneven all-Asia picture contains clear indications of the following: the extreme weakness of the South Asian region; a qualitative gap between South Asia and South-East Asia; and the momentum (in systemic terms) gained during the last two decades by North and North-East Asia in general, and China in particular. South Asian countries have only recently begun to emerge gradually from a long night of darkness, symbolised by the India-Pakistan Pyrrhic conflict and India's repeated attempts to dominate the region, into a new era marked by less mutual suspicion, if not greater mutual trust.

This slow change has been signalled by the evolution of the South Asian Association for Regional Co-operation (SAARC), since its inception in 1983, into a forum for discussions of common problems of the region, and a scaling down of India's ambitions through the adumbration of a new line of approach to regional issues embodied in the 'Gujral doctrine'.[4]

Even so, the SAARC is a far weaker inter-governmental body than ASEAN, and lags behind the latter in the economic promise that it holds for the future - although it is true that both share the same kind of allergy to democratic politics. The weakness of the SAARC in general, and India (as its largest member) in particular, is highlighted by the fact that whereas ASEAN invites China and Japan to attend its meetings on trade, to date India has not been able to secure similar recognition of its international status as an Asian power. Thus, in such shifts of power as may now be under way between Asia and the West, South Asia will remain relatively weak in the emerging pecking order to which globalisation will eventually lead.

The role of social science

The second strand of this discussion relates to the insufficient role played by the social sciences during the last three decades in providing the basis for an

---

4. During the intervals within which the Congress (I) was not the ruling party at the centre, foreign ministers A.B.Vajpayee and I.K.Gujral altered the style and substance of India's foreign policy marginally for the better.

understanding of the complex political processes in which the phenomena of development and underdevelopment are embedded. Social science can contribute to new initiatives in the related spheres of reduction of poverty and empowerment of the weaker segments of society only by a radical alteration of the structure and content of its discourse. It ought to start with an explicit recognition of the roots of mass poverty in the rapacious exploitation arising out of the combination of global capitalism, imperial power, and of state power dominated by different segments of indigenous capital.

Social science discourse should provide more space for the exploration of participatory democracy instead of concentrating on the virtues of good governance, invoking the salience of 'security' (i.e. the preservation of the status quo), and placing the 'state' as the centrepiece of discussions of development and change. Research ought to focus greater attention on the contrast between autonomy and competition (which lies at the heart of capitalist economic development), and the new enterprise of complementation and co-operation (without which poverty cannot be eradicated and 'security' in its deepest sense cannot be guaranteed) between different segments of any given society, between different societies in any given region, and between region and region.

Development theory, as it emerged in academic institutions, revolved round the tension between three major pairs of concepts: in economics, between growth and development; in politics, between state and society; and, in sociology, between tradition and modernity. The social scientific study of the Third World was premised on: (1) a mechanical application to newly-independent countries of the methodology of study, and of research findings, derived from the advanced political economies of the West, with an emphasis placed on the comparative dimension; and (2) implicitly, if not explicitly, discrediting all attempts to develop models other than the Western bourgeois path.

Linearity and reductionism, research by extrapolation from the experience of the past in Western Europe and of the present and future in non-Western countries, a mechanical imposition of the Weberian paradigm and transfer of bourgeois democratic institutions, and a vigorous export of the model of urbanisation, industrialisation and modernisation, without proper attention being given to the grave problems of survival and poverty faced by the rural masses, constituted the intellectual foundation of mainstream development studies.

Academic obsession with the state as the ensemble of structures of power at the core of the emerging institutions of government led to a neglect of political processes which often side-stepped formal channels or quite simply took place in extra-institutional spaces; nor have academics paid attention to local history. With a few exceptions, academic writing has neglected the negative impact of the operation of state power on the economic condition of the mass of the people; and most scholars have shown scant awareness of the extent to which even very poor people in the Third World are conscious of their democratic, civil and human rights and freedoms.

Within the social science disciplines, especially economics, politics and sociology, the study of problems and their solutions, the study of policies and projects, and the identification of new areas of research at the macroscopic level, were almost always carried out at the expense of the microscopic, and often also at the expense of intermediate levels as well. The same mindset prevailed when the sights were lowered, towards the end of the 1960s, in order to look at small-scale problems on a regional or sub-regional rather than the national level. Empirical questions continued to be posed with reference to elites, institutionally channelled power, and local administration as the microcosm of the national government, rather than with reference to the problems faced by different segments of the population in whose midst poverty was being produced, reproduced and intensified.

South Asia is particularly vulnerable to an intensification of mass poverty: the states in the region (including the Indian state) are severely handicapped by their dual character, i.e. hard on the interior and soft on the exterior. On the one hand, they treat harshly domestic demands for a policy of fairer and more equitable distribution and reduction of poverty, bringing the full coercive weight of the state apparatus to bear on the deprived and aggrieved sections of society.[5] On the other, they are too impotent to withstand the tight embrace of globalisation and maintain their autonomy even in a relative sense. The political compromises that they make invariably benefit the different segments of the dominant classes at the expense of the weaker segments of society.

---

5. It is useful to remember that South Asia and sub-Saharan Africa are closely similar in respect of their poverty levels. See Jean Drèze and Amartya Sen (eds), *India: Economic Development and Social Opportunity*, OUP Oxford and Delhi; and *Indian Development: Selected Regional Perspectives*, 1997.

Thus, for example, an interesting contrast between China and India suggests itself. The modernisation/globalisation project has given rise to an uneven growth of poverty in China. This is a novel experience for China, which the Chinese state claims that it can handle by confining poverty to peripheral regions and monitoring it carefully, whilst letting the hinterland (between and around the two great rivers, and along the eastern seaboard) develop at a great speed. At least a part of the logic underlying China's policy would appear to rest on the state (and not foreign powers or the World Bank or the IMF) determining the pace of globalisation and the level of involvement that it would allow to foreign governments and investors. In stark contrast to China, India has shown itself utterly unable to resist pressure from the World Bank, the IMF and the West to get on with globalisation according to a formula pushed by them. This is partly because India has, over the years, become severely indebted, and also, even more importantly perhaps, because its development policies in the past have led to an intensification rather than an alleviation of poverty.

Political and economic polarisation

During the last two decades, two parallel processes have gathered momentum in South Asia. The dominant classes (a much more apt term than either the 'ruling classes' or 'elites') have undergone a process of differentiation and proliferation. As a political reflection of this process, state power has increasingly come under the control of coalitions between parties representing different class segments, thus putting an end to one-party dominance under civilian rule, or military government, as the case may be.

Power-sharing, or alternation in power between parties representing different segments of the dominant classes, has become more the rule than the exception. In a large country such as India, the political power-sharing experiment had its beginning at the state level and spread to the centre after a brief interval. In smaller countries, power-sharing, as in Nepal, was introduced at the central level, with minute doses of devolution down to the lowest or *panchayat* level. In general, the Westminster model has been flexibly re-moulded (though less impressively in cases such as Sri Lanka) to take account of this process of differentiation, despite the fact that control over state structures is conditioned by inescapable refractions of class identity through the prisms of social, regional, communal and gender-based differentiations.

Two prevailing modalities of wielding power in the region can be gleaned from the concrete experience of South Asian states during the last half century. I shall refer here to three examples of this general phenomenon. In Pakistan, the military usurped power from a weak and venal civilian state and imposed a near-absolute rule, interrupted from time to time by brief and erratic bouts of elected civilian administration under notoriously corrupt political parties. India experienced, for well over four decades, one-party dominance at the centre under Congress rule. The major project of the Congress Party was to bend the constitution in such ways as would guarantee a maximum centralisation of state power and justify the imposition of a basically anti-people rule, that benefited (to differing degrees) the different fractions of a proliferating bourgeoisie.[6] In Sri Lanka, which began its career with the nearest approximation to the Westminster model of bourgeois democratic government in the region, the process of centralisation of power that gathered pace during the 1970s so completely transformed the political experience of the mass of the people that within a brief interval the demand for fission by the Tamil Elam forces became as irrevocable as the government's determination to suppress it.

The other modality of power has resulted from the failure of centralisation of state power to contain the internal contradictions between the different dominant class fractions caused by divisions of a horizontal nature. In Pakistan, over-centralisation of power assumed such proportions as to reduce the eastern part of the country to the level of an internal colony leading to a war of secession. Even after the severance of Bangladesh, Pakistan has persisted in centralising power with predictably destabilising consequences. In Afghanistan, external intervention destroyed a relatively progressive centralised administration and created conditions under which a prolonged alternation between tyranny and anarchy has become unavoidable.

In India, Congress rule was successfully challenged by regional forces as well as agrarian interests (with an overlap between the two). Since the

---

6. T.V. Sathyamurthy, 'The constitution as an instrument of political coercion in post-colonial states: the case of India 1950-1993', in Abdo I. Baaklini and Helen Desfosses (eds), *Designs for Democratic Stability: studies for viable constitutionalism*, Sharpe, Armonk, NY 1997, pp147-78.

Internal Emergency (1975-77) and the breaking of the Congress Party's monopoly over state power, the party system has undergone a radical change, with no single party large enough or sufficiently strong to dominate the centre. Coalition rule at the centre and in the states has become the norm. Decentralisation of power-wielding structures from the centre to the district and below has followed, rather than an attempt to prevent the proliferation of (refracted) class forces at different levels of society. This does not mean that state power so devolved is fundamentally democratic (i.e. essentially pro-people) in character.

Even more serious, for its long-term political consequences, is the process of polarisation between rich and poor which has gathered pace in recent decades. This polarisation cuts across other social divides: communal, gender, and social-hierarchical. Its impact has been phenomenal and holds the promise of catastrophe for the future. Polarisation between the rich and the poor is a process from which there are few exceptions. Even in China, the recent lurch of the economy has added vastly to the ranks of the poor (350 million, or 30 per cent of the population, according to certain estimates), whilst intensifying the differentiation between economically successful and backward regions. No study of international relations can afford to ignore the long-term impact of this phenomenon. In the domestic sphere, the political fall-out from economic polarisation has assumed the form of severe erosion of legitimacy of the state, especially in the eyes of the poor. The rift between the dominant classes and the vast mass of agricultural and urban poor - a rift that is a direct outcome of policies adopted by successive post-colonial governments even before the onset of the effects of globalisation - has a significance even greater than the threat of ethnic separatism, or communalism rooted in religious differences.

The major impact of globalisation consists of an intensification of 'democratic deficit' (in civil 'democratic' regimes) or authoritarian misrule (in military and other forms of undemocratic rule), as the case may be. As the focus shifts away from the condition of the mass of the people towards meeting economic criteria favourable to investment, markets, profits and privatisation, even the little that used to be done for the alleviation of poverty goes by default. The World Bank's recent conversion to a poverty-sensitive stance in its dealings with the countries of the region is meretricious to say the least. Were the Bank to apply its own anti-poverty criteria rigorously, poverty would intensify even further than at present because investment-starved economies invariably blame and punish the poor for their misfortunes.

The importance of participatory democracy

There would appear to be only one way open to the peoples of these societies to break out of the vicious circle of skewed development, and of the damaging consequences of the unholy matrimony between the forces of globalising capitalism and the dominant classes in the host societies. That would be to forge alternative modes of democratically based participatory political action and to create conditions (including new structures) favourable to a pattern of socio-economic behaviour responsive to ordinary human values.[7] There is no dearth of ideas that could provide an ideological basis for such a transformation. Thus it is not surprising that Gandhi's ideas on education, trusteeship and self-sufficient (and indeed autochthonous) development have worked their way into many a grass-root movement in India during the last quarter of a century. The fact that, by and large, movements of resistance have not assumed a confrontational stance in their struggles against structures of centralising power should not mislead us into underestimating their transformational potential, at least in the medium run, for herein lies the path to survival.

In South Asia, as elsewhere in the third world, the experience of oppression has been palpable. It has taken the form of vast swathes of the population living below the poverty line, their lives utterly insecure, robbed of dignity, and subject to malnutrition, illiteracy, exploitation of female and child labour, and a number of other deprivations of fundamental human needs. In other words, the price of the distorted development of Third World societies, and the costs incurred by willing indigenous/national governments toeing the line of foreign capital and international finance, are being borne by the poorer sections of their societies.

By the same token, these governments are now no longer in a position to use the flimsy excuse of support from a non-existent Soviet Union as a

---

7. There is of course a whole separate argument relating to 'sustainability'.

countervailing justification for their profoundly anti-people policies. In India, for example, large masses of the poor (at a rough estimate, 45 per cent of a current population of nearly one billion) are merely existing, surviving from one day to the next, submerged beneath the poverty line drawn by the government itself. And an even worse fate has befallen countries caught up in persistent cycles of famine, drought and internecine wars. The sum of human misery seems to accumulate without limit.

Under these conditions, state structures have ceased to touch the welfare of large sections of the population. And, when they do come into contact with the lives of the people, the message is one of doom rather than relief.

Uneven and truncated development, under such unfavourable conditions of accumulation, has contributed to a sea change in the conditions of living in the urban and rural working masses. The development of the Indian working class has been interrupted by the shifting economic strategy of the state, whose principal aim (since the early 1970s) has become one of shoring up a dependent bourgeois capitalist class by increasing repression of the organised sector of the working class, marginalising large segments of it, attacking the security of conditions of work, restricting democratic liberties and elementary civil rights, and standing by, if not actually colluding with, the rich and middle peasants' repression of the poor peasantry and agricultural labour.

The social hypertrophy resulting from the expansion of the ranks of the poor has brought politicians in general, and the political system as a whole, increasingly into disrepute. Civil society is at a crossroads, with the increased expectations of certain upwardly mobile segments of the rising classes coming directly into conflict with the minimal requirements of survival of the mass of the population.

The problematic character of class struggle in India (in contrast to, say, China) has been inescapable, given the newly emerging character of the capitalist and proletarian classes at Independence. The proliferation of the former and the fragmentation of the latter have followed complex paths and become interwoven with other sociological (i.e. ethnic, caste, regional, communal, cultural and gender) categories that have appeared in different idiomatic versions in different contexts.

To a large extent, although by no means entirely, this particular path of development can be understood in terms of the uneven and dependent character of the Indian capitalist project.[8] The chief sufferers in the experiment of squeezing capitalist relations of production into the interstices of a social formation (wrongly dismissed as 'Asiatic Mode of Production' by certain brands of reductionists) which is still closely interwoven with pre-capitalist relations of production (especially in agriculture) have been the mass of the Indian people. With even left-wing parties sucked into the project of establishing an underdeveloped and lopsided form of capitalist development after abandoning their original strategy, the weaker sections of Indian society have had to fend for themselves and fight off the repressive encroachments of the Indian state and the day-to-day political, economic, cultural and social oppression to which the dominant segments of society subject them. From the 1970s onwards, mass organisations and grass-roots movements have increasingly come to the fore, precisely with such a purpose in view.

Grass-roots movements

Let us pause to consider the ways in which the poor defend themselves. Although they appear to be defenceless at the macroscopic (i.e. national) or even intermediate (i.e. regional and sub-regional) levels, they have nevertheless shown themselves to be capable of identifying issues that affect their survival. They have demonstrated their ability to organise themselves to resist the encroachment of a variety of forces (unleashed by the state, by rapacious politicians, by industry and by modern agriculture, to mention only a few examples) on vital resources on which their livelihood depends. These include

---

8. It is often taken for granted that, because the market has expanded during the past forty years, great strides have been made in the sphere of economic development. The dark side of this truism is seldom analysed. It is true that the market has expanded beyond all expectation in India - (in terms of rough but reasonable magnitude) from about 25 per cent of the population during the early 1950s (75 million) to about 75 per cent of the population in the 1980s and 1990s (say 600 million). What this kind of assertion omits is that, compared with nearly 200 million people who were not touched by the market at independence (when the non monetary sector was less restrictive than it is today), more than 300 million have now sunk to such a low level of poverty that they are untouched by the market, or are only on its outermost fringes. See T.V. Sathyamurthy (ed), *Social Change and Political Discourse in India: Structures of Power, Movements Of Resistance. Vol.3: Region, Religion, Caste, Gender and Culture in Contemporary India* and Volume 4: *Class Formation and Political Transformation In Post Colonial India*, OUP, Oxford and Delhi 1996.

forests, natural sources of energy and water and subsistence agriculture. They have come to realise, over the decades, not only that they cannot rely on the state to defend their environment and the meagre material base on which they have to fashion their life and survival strategies, but also that the state itself is a formidable obstacle capable of mobilising its coercive power in ways that undermine them.

The intervention of the poor in politics as a measure of self defence has led to a political transformation in identifiable spheres, as a consequence of the working out of the dialectic between a coercive state enmeshed in the horizontal division of the bourgeoisie (or dominant classes), on the one hand, and on the other a public that has become more and more democratically orientated at the grass-roots level. One of the most significant developments in India since the Internal Emergency (1975-77) consists of the surfacing of a politics of the people for a safer and better environment; for safeguarding hard-won human rights resisting the violence of the state (either as a pro-active agent or in collusion with dominant castes, landed interests, industrial employers and/or communal elements); for a population policy essentially pro-people in character; for education more responsive to all their needs; and, above all, for a civil society in which the 'weaker segments' could feel reasonably secure.

In a number of areas, and in the context of state policies jeopardising their livelihood in the name of development, the poor have had to rely on their own slender resources in order to wage political struggles leading to self-empowerment and to increased chances of protecting the communal sources of food, energy, water and air on which they depend for their survival. During the last twenty years, nearly three thousand struggles of this kind have been waged throughout the length and breadth of the country. These have involved people living under different conditions of deprivation, and spread over fairly substantial areas. In some instances, as in the *chipko andolan* (originating, in this case, in north-eastern Uttar Pradesh in the district of Clumoli) to protect trees, the experience gained in one area led to the rise of similar struggles in a number of other areas (e.g. Himachal Pradesh in the north-west, and Karnataka in the south).

The *chipko andolan* can reasonably be regarded as representing an acute form of dissent arising out of the concrete experience of those affected by the government's policy of denying natural resources to rural dwellers whose survival depends upon access to them, while allowing those very resources to be appropriated by private entrepreneurs. Such struggles invariably give rise to complex interplays of contradictory forces.

Faced with such novel forms of struggle, the state resorts to a multiplicity of tactics to contain or divert the agents of change. Among the means employed by the state towards such an end are suppression, appropriation and structural change. By the same token, its increased visibility (not only locally, but also nationally and internationally) and public profile tend to divert the movement from its quintessentially agrarian and peasant character.

The experience of mass mobilisations, such as the *chipko andolan*, points to ways in which the mass of the working people gain the experience of self-government, self-management and self-administration that will enable them ultimately to create a society in their own image: one that is based on co-operation rather than competition, equality and mutuality rather than dominion and subordination, production for need rather than production for profit.

In order to advance towards such a goal, educational and cultural policies should lay emphasis on the needs of the mass of the people. In other words, they should be given the opportunity to benefit from a proletarian education and culture responsive to the needs and aspirations of the mass of the people. One indication of the failure of the left to achieve this goal is the persistence of high levels of illiteracy; another, the growing menace of communalism.

E ducation has been used effectively as a means of advancement by the upwardly mobile strata of society, both urban and rural; but the majority of children still fail to complete even elementary or primary education. The reasons for this neglect range from the undoubted lack of availability of education to the widespread prevalence of poverty and child labour. But there is also the problem of lack of motivation, because education is often not seen by the poor as something that contributes in any way to a gain in understanding of, and control over, their environment, and this is a consequence of the type of education provided, with its alien class content.

Despite its innovative character and higher international visibility, the *chipko andolan* shares several similarities with other protest movements (e.g. the *Narmada Bachao andolan*, the Jharkhand agitation, and the Baliapal struggle). But the specificity of each struggle is crucial to the decoding of the political transformation under way in India. Thus, for example, each movement develops its own antibodies in order to resist appropriation, leading to a greater or lesser immunity to this particular form of neutralisation. At the same time, the range of issues addressed by such movements has expanded over the years to include not only causes of immediate material interest, crucial as they are, but also issues relating to the civic, democratic and human rights of the mass of the people.

The legitimacy, if not the credibility, of the hegemonic order has been dented. In the resulting crisis, stability and order can no longer be taken for granted. The mass of the people (consisting of economically and socially disadvantaged sections) has

> 'An original commitment to liberal values has degenerated into conflicts between and within classes'

come to see the state as an instrument of power which the richer/dominant sections of society manipulate to their own advantage and which the poorer or 'weaker' sections should resist in order to survive. Civil society is thus at a crossroads in South Asia, increasingly engulfed in violence.

In a fundamental sense, the current crisis in India is due to the failure of the Indian state and national bourgeoisie to establish fully capitalist relations of production within a bourgeois democratic public framework. An original commitment to liberal values and to forging a model of society capable of combining equality (as reflected in 'the socialistic pattern of society') with liberty and justice (i.e. the enjoyment of civil, democratic, fundamental, and human rights as the basis of a stable system of law and order equally applicable to all segments of society), has degenerated into conflicts both across class barriers and within classes.

The initiative for restoring social balance and for transforming the political system is no longer with the political parties, but with the mass of the people taking up specific issues in particular regions. It is therefore important to distinguish between mass politics (and agitations) and civil violence (and anarchy) in order to appreciate the differences between the political initiatives of the poor and the workings of a system of political parties increasingly criminalised through their dependence on anti-social and lumpen elements.

The challenge of globalisation

I have not so far considered the challenges arising out of pressures generated by globalisation. With the end of the cold war and the demise of the Soviet Union, the 1990s have witnessed policies of wholesale totalisation thrust upon governments of all political hues, by the combined strength of the forces of imperialism under the leadership of the USA and the economically near-omnipotent institutions embodying the interests of global capital, *viz* the multi- and trans-nationals, the World Bank, the IMF and their adjuncts. One of the consequences of this new surge of world capitalism has been to introduce even greater distortions into the politics of third world states. If, in our understanding of what the word 'politics' means, we include the economic, social and democratic welfare of the people, these new developments portend problems at two major levels.

Globalisation involves greater competition for new markets between those controlling different segments of capital and extending the frontiers of capitalist production, and radical hegemonic shifts that are bound to alter power balances between regions of the world and within individual regions. Inter-regional transformations and intra-regional adjustments will almost certainly introduce new configurations of power. This is indeed a subject fraught with tension and full of possibilities for intelligent speculation about what the future holds. I shall not comment on this aspect of globalisation here.

For social scientists, globalisation provides yet another opportunity to raise hitherto neglected problems for future study. What ought to be the focus for social science research? How should students of politics view the question of interdisciplinary work? Amartya Sen and Jean Drèze have single-mindedly addressed the question of what focus social science research should adopt. Their contribution to the study of development has enriched not only economics but also philosophy.

Their work on India, and Amartya Sen's comparative examination of different human, social, political and international contexts of chronic deprivation such as droughts and famines, have enriched conceptual vocabulary and research methodology with inter-linkages between politics, economics and philosophy that have put new flesh on fundamentally important ideas such as 'entitlement to basic fulfillments' and social opportunities. But, unfortunately, despite their highly significant contribution to our understanding of the dynamic economic development under democratic conditions, they have not challenged - certainly not explicitly challenged - the privileging of the state in social science research.

The privileging of the political over the economic in the study of the structures of power would necessarily involve an examination of the means available to political movements/institutions to resist the globalisation which the state promotes. At the same time, it would also involve a privileging within the political realm of popular movements of resistance over the quotidian interventions of well-heeled political organisations patronising the poor.

Let us return to the theme of democracy. An irreproachable exercise in electoral democracy may well constitute a tiny first step along the road to substantive democracy.

Participatory democracy is still a long way off, however, though India's advance from electoral democracy is a necessary condition for its realisation. Systematic analytic treatment of the relationship between the electoral, substantive and participatory aspects of democracy (in general as well as in the Indian political context) is thin on the ground. Students of politics tend to concentrate on these closely interwoven strands in isolation from one another rather than as integral parts of the same phenomenon. The distinction that I have in mind here is between these three aspects of democracy:

1) Electoral democracy, which constitutes the most elementary and necessary but by no means sufficient condition for the functioning of democracy.
2) Substantive democracy, which constitutes opportunities for the people to act institutionally in times of crisis in order to remove threats to the constitutional guarantees of democratic choice (e.g. after the Internal Emergency of 1975-77).
3) Participatory democracy, which goes beyond the institutional confines into the more complex terrain of the mass of the people taking part in politics in order to influence if not shape public policy.

The tension between the three waves of democratic political activity at the level of the mass of the people is further heightened by the submergence of large segments of rural and urban population below the poverty line, with the struggle as the only means by which they can make themselves heard. The sheer numbers involved renders this an all but insurmountable problem.

We should be under no illusion that a relatively clean election will automatically lead to a reversal of the economic hardship that liberalisation has brought to the mass of the Indian people. That end can only be achieved by sustained popular and mass resistance, and by forging a clear alternative vision.

To conclude, we may well be on the cusp in the study of politics, on the verge of a new phase in which greater emphasis will be laid on political processes, representing a radical shift in focus. We are witnessing a steady, albeit painful, evolution of forms of political participation involving different segments of the mass of the population, with the accompanying requirement that institutions should adapt themselves to political necessity, rather than that the participatory urge of the people having should be modified or diluted in order that they conform to the mores of the dominant institutions of state and society.

Social science can contribute to new initiatives in the related terrains of reduction of poverty and empowerment of weaker segments of society, and can play a significant role by radically altering the structure and content of its discourse. It ought to start with an explicit recognition of the roots of mass impoverishment and immiseration in the rapacious exploitation arising out of the penetration of a combination of forces: of global capitalism, of far-flung imperialist power and of state power dominated by different indigenous segments of capital throughout the world.

Social science disciplines would benefit from providing more space and resources for the exploration of participatory democracy starting with the grass roots, instead of concentrating on the modalities and virtues of 'good governance'. Research should focus attention on the contradiction between the anatomy of competition (lying at the heart of capitalist development) and the new enterprise of co-operation and complementarity between different segments of society.

Conscript

A story

Kevin Parry

'*Saamsmelt!*' bellows the sergeant. '*Julle moet saam met die landskap smelt!*' (Merge!
You must merge with the landscape!)

I lie face down, exhausted, gasping the detested red dust deep into my lungs. In
the sky the sun is an incandescent disc of platinum, filling the valley with
claustrophobic heat. No river ever ran here; rain on this scorched landscape is
unimaginable. The sparse clumps of khaki grass, the olive-grey scrub bushes
with their harsh Afrikaans names - *karoobos, bitterbos, spekboom, vygie* - seem to
expect of the barren sky and of the baked red earth, nothing. The crippled thorn
trees spread their claws to the sky in fertile supplication. What survives here
does so only by self-mutilation, leaves deformed into stumps, and roots into
tubers. Here they subsist with as little point or hope as the blistering iron boulders
and heat-fractured shards that litter the landscape.

'*Saamsmelt, saamsmelt, jull' vuilgoed!*' (Merge, merge, you trash!)

The guttural barks hang upon the heat, the language congruent with the
landscape it names and claims, each phoneme a rock, a shard, a broken carapace.
Congruent, too, are the conscripts, mostly Afrikaners, from *Uitenage, De Aar,
Graaff-Reinet, Burgersdorp, Dordrecht*. Impervious as iguana skin to the searing
sun, their bodies tan olive, burnt umber, black-brown, the colour of biltong, of
wildebeest hide. Seemingly as indigenous as the fauna, as the rust-brown lizards,
locusts, tuberous puff-adders, they are absorbed in this myth-ghosted terrain of
ancestral Boer heroism, resilience and retribution, this landscape over which

seems to hover the brutal guardians of the Afrikaner soul - Kruger, Malan, Verwoerd, Vorster.

Sweat, dripping from my nose and chin, rolls into little balls in the dust, which will not absorb it, and my heart pounds against the stunting mantle of this disclaimed motherland. My antipathy is retributed by the sun, which has burned my fair skin crimson, raised it in great watery blisters and left my face a mass of porous raw meat, stinging at the touch of the sun, of the air as I move, of the salt courses of my sweat. Like an allergen this place acts upon me, cauterising my flesh, insinuating into my bloodstream the thin toxins which would desiccate and twist into thorns the leaves of my soul but which cannot prevail against the copious serum of my hatred, my antidote against despair. I will not be assimilated, I will not submit.

Drowsy waves of noise undulate from all quarters. I lie on my bed, reading, trying to shut out the ebb and flow and staccato of banality. In one corner of the bungalow a group of conscripts plays poker on a metal trunk; across the way someone strums and continually readjusts the tuning on a guitar; near the door a large group listens to an olive-skinned 'ou man' with oily black hair who has just returned from the border and fields dramatic accounts of near-contacts with terrorists, daring escapades, sadistic officers, riotous booze-ups and how we are going to '*affkak*' (shit off) in the bush. Over all this drifts the syrupy voice of the Forces Favourites radio presenter and the insipid bilingual messages: 'To Marty and Flip and all the *ou manne* at the *Voortrekkerhoogte ... min dae, julle* (few days, all of you) ... don't forget your promise, darling ... *geluk op jou verjaardsdag, Hannie* (good luck on your birthday) ... every cloud has a silver lining ... *ons is baie trots op jou, Boet* (we are very proud of you) ... and for all of you, here's Jim Reeves with ...' Others sit about in ones and twos, talking, polishing belts, buckles, badges, writing letters, cleaning rifles, smoking, staring into space. Infusing every sound, pervasive as the heat, is ennui. I hold my book close to my face, parrying distraction, fencing myself in behind the barbed black strands of printed lines, muffling the din with the insulating white spaces of the page. I roll each word about in thought, feeling its globular fullness, its form and texture, coating it as a protective bubble of amber, so that the images and sounds might drop down pure and pearl-like into my mind.

I am suddenly startled by silence. Everyone is standing to attention. At the foot of my bed stands a lieutenant, pencil-line moustache, two pips, permanent-force. I put my book down and jump to attention. The conscripts titter.

'*Nou ja. Watter kak is dit wat so belangwekkend is?*' (Yes, now. What shit is this that is so interesting?) he says, picking up my open book. Aloud, he laboriously begins to plough the sentences, his heavy accent turning the words like clods:

The soul walks not upon a line, neither does it grow like a reed.
The soul unfolds itself, like a lotus of countless petals.

In slow, exaggerated disbelief he shakes his head, saying ponderously, 'My - Here - God!' (My - Lord - God!) The conscripts take the cue and guffaw. I keep my eyes fixed forward, will not smile.

He turns to the title page. 'The Prophet. *Ja, nee. Is jy no 'n* 'prophet', *ou maat?* Huh?' (Are you a prophet, old mate?) I say nothing. He looks up at me, eyebrows raised, demanding an answer. 'No, sir.'

'*Ka ...wat? Kah ... Kahlil Gibral. God is dit nou 'n vokken kaffer of 'n Indier of wat?*' (God, now is this a fucking kaffir or an Indian or what?)

Some of the conscripts snicker. I remain at attention, silent.

'*Ek jet jou iets gevraaaaaa. Verstaan jy Afrikaans?*' (I asked you something. Do you understand Afrikaans?)

'Yes, Sir.'

'*Nou ja, antwoord my. Is dit 'n blerrie kaffer wat jy lees?*'

'No Sir; he's Lebanese.'

'*O, 'n Arabier, huh? Nou hoekom lees jy nie Afrikaanse boeke nie? Mmmmmh?*' (Oh, an Arab? How come you don't read Afrikaans books?)

I remain impassive, eyes front.

'*Kan jy Afrikaans praat?*' (Can you speak Afrikaans?)

'Yes, Sir.'

'*Vaarom dan antwoord jy my nie in Afrikaans nie?*' (Why then don't you answer me in Afrikaans?)

'I am English, Sir.'

'English!' he bellows. '*Jy's 'n Suid Afrikaner, is jy nie?*' (English! You're a South African, aren't you?)

'I'm English-speaking, Sir.'

He puts his face close to mine, slitting his eyes. 'Well you, Mister Englishman, you just better watch your footsteps round here, hey. Because why, I'm gonna be watching you. *Word net die wit man met my en ek gaan jou vokken naai. He jy my?*' (Just act the white man with me and I'm going to fucking screw you. Have you got me?)

———

In the shade of the kitchen verandah I sit with two Afrikaner fatigues around a huge aluminium pot, peeling sacks of potatoes. Through the open windows drifts the lurch and swing of *Boeremusik*, depressingly gay accordion dance music and cloying ballads. Intermittently this is interrupted by the announcement of the election results. Like the granite blocks of a wall, inexorably, the National Party victories stack up.

'*Nog 'n een!*' (Another one!) shout the two Afrikaners in unison, and each hurls a potato splashing into the brimming pot. Similar yelps of joy and whistling erupt in the kitchen.

'*Hoe se jy, ou kafferboetie?*' (What do you say, old kaffir-brother?) they mock in glee.

'Helen!' I respond each time, and hurl my own potato smashing into the water. The lonely Progressive seat of Mrs Suzman was announced last night, a tiny star to cling to in the darkness, a small pool of shade in the sterile wasteland.

'*Ag, pateties, man. Jy en jou Peter Hain, Jy's 'n vokken verraaier*' (Ag, pathetic, man. You and your Peter Hain, you're a fucking traitor).

'Traitor to what?'

'*Onse land*' (Our country).

'Fuck you, I'm true to myself.'

At the corner of the kitchen block a Landrover draws up. The driver, a P.F. corporal, shouts to someone round the corner, '*Jy! Bring twee van dae manne*' (You! Bring two of those men) and reverses down the concrete driveway towards the steps where we are sitting. As he halts, two black convicts appear from around the corner, followed by a short old Coloured guard in a greatcoat much too long for him. The guard carries a short spear and a knobkerrie and clucks at them, '*Maak gou, baleka, baleka, kom jong!*' (Hurry up!). The driver gets out and drops the tailgate. '*Haal hom uit*' (pull it out), he snaps at the convicts. They wear shabby black shirts and outsize khaki shorts which cover their knees. Their thin black shanks are dusty and their feet bare. They reach into the back of the vehicle and tug out by the rear legs a huge dead pig. The long carcass hits the concrete with the hard hollow sound of a falling log. The driver slams shut the tailgate and drives away.

The guard and convicts stand around the carcass, staring down at it. The three of us, sitting round the pot of potatoes, stare at it too. It is a huge beast, about six feet long, narrow-backed and surprisingly long-legged. The bristled skin is mainly flesh-coloured but is mottled here and there with large pastel-mauve patches which seem to lie just beneath the skin, like contusions, as though the animal had been beaten before death. The closed eyes are delicately fringed with long, blonde, human-like lashes.

The kitchen sergeant, pot-bellied and ruddy-faced, emerges in his short white coat and walks over to the carcass. He kicks it lightly in the ribs. '*Aai, maar di's nou 'n groote, né?'* (It's a big one, hey?) He stands there with his boot on the beast's side, like a victorious hunter, rocking it gently. *'Ja, sy's 'n groote, my baas, 'n groote'* (Yes, she's a big one, my boss) drools the toothless old guard, sucking his rubbery pink lips in and out. On the lapel of his greatcoat is a frayed band of Coloured Corps service ribbons from the last war.

The sergeant walks round the carcass, flaps the long ear with his boot, kicks the front trotters, lifts the kinked tail. He stares at the pig's backside. 'Christus!' he says and shoots us a crude grin. The conscripts laugh throatily. He turns to the little ancient guard and points at the pig's pudenda. *'Daar's jou laaste kans, ou Piet'* (There's your last chance, old Piet), he says. *'Nee, nee, my baas, nee, Jusus!'* (No, no my boss, no, Jesus!) giggles the old guard.

The sergeant turns to the convicts. *'Ina'* (here), he says sternly, pointing between them and the pig's backside. They look at him solemnly, with apparent incomprehension. *'Kom, kom, wie's eerste?'* (Come, come, who's first?) he says, smacking his fist repeatedly into his open palm and lifting the pig's tail with the toe of his boot. The convicts make low confused exclamations. One shakes his head with the glimmer of an obsequious smile and begins to shuffle awkwardly on his big calloused feet; the other stands still, looking down at the ground.

'God, word die kaffers wit of is hulle net vokken dom? Ina, jul' bliksems' (God, are these kaffirs getting white or are they just fucking dumb. Here, you scoundrels) the sergeant says, and begins to pump his hips in extravagant mock copulation. The conscripts, and some of the kitchen staff who have gathered round, hoot and guffaw. The shuffling convict continues his nervous little dance and broadens his fawning smile; the other remains still, with his head down, but I am jolted to see that his eyes, staring up from beneath his brows, are now fixed directly on me.

'Kom, jong' the sergeant growls, continuing to pump his hips, *'moenie voorgee nie dat jul' blerrie swartes nie lus vir 'n bietjie lekker pink doos is nie'* (Come, don't pretend you bloody blacks don't lust after a bit of luscious pink cunt). The stare of the taller convict, dark and expressionless, remains unwaveringly on me; the other has put his palms together and is chanting softly, *'O, lung'wam, O my groot baas'* ('Oh, my big white boss').

The sergeant throws his hands up in feigned exasperation. *'Di's nou dankbaarheid, né? Kom, jul' lelike bobbejane - binnekant!'* (Now, that's gratitude, hey? Come, you ugly baboons - inside!) he says, his face scarlet with exertion, his paunch quivering with mirth, and follows the convicts as they stagger up the stairs towards the kitchen door, the dead beast on their shoulders. As they pass, the convict at the rear, hunched under the weight of the big human-pink carcass, fixes me again with his indecipherable eyes. Close up, I see the whites are jaundiced and shot with blood.

The two fatigues chuckle on about the sergeant for a while and we settle back into the monotony of the potatoes. Above the mindless scraping, between the flitting of thoughts, the *Boeresmusik* reasserts itself, repetitious phrases flouncing like long white skirts and bobbing bonnets, the saccharine sentiments of insularity, the strident rhythms of the laager.

––––––

She turns towards me, hair across her face, but her achingly impossible presence becomes confused with the numb ring of exhaustion in my head as my bed is jolted by kicks.

'*Vok jou drome, roof. Staan op!*' (Fuck your dreams, scab. Get up!)

I sit up in slow automation, registering the lieutenant's voice. The dark bungalow is freezing. I keep my eyes shut but cannot retrieve her image from the sanctuary of my sleep. My damp socks stick uncomfortably to my feet from sleeping with my boots on. Guards are not permitted to remove their boots and I've had mine on for over thirty hours: two hours on duty, three hours off. I feel for my greatcoat in the darkness and haul it on, wincing as the rough collar raps my sunburned neck. In the bed next to me someone mutters unintelligibly and turns over. The coffee left in the cistern is barely tepid, but I swallow half a mugful.

'*Tree aan*' (fall in) the lieutenant says.

I put on my helmet, take my rifle and follow the other three guards out of the bungalow. The night is still and wrenchingly cold and the crunching of our boots on the gravel as we fall in beneath the stars is like the sound of ice breaking. The lieutenant brings us to attention and we march towards the perimeter watchtowers that overlook the security precinct. The strike of our boots beats back sharply at us as we pass between the rows of barracks, but is suddenly dissipated as we emerge onto the vast tarmac area of the transport section. As the silhouettes of the armoured-vehicle hangars recede on our left the moon emerges. It is gibbous. Beneath it, the comet remains a red gash. Between the tarmac expanse and the boundless night sky we march like clockwork miniatures.

I am stationed in the tower furthest from the guardhouse. After the guard has been changed in the third tower, the lieutenant orders the retiring guards back to the guardhouse, then quick-marches me alone towards the northern tower. He remains behind me. Our steps beat together. My breath steams out into the frosty air. Suddenly, as the silhouette of the tower comes into view, he orders me to halt. We are still about a hundred yards from the tower, too far away even for the guard to challenge us. I halt and stand there to attention, waiting. The lieutenant remains behind me, how close I cannot tell, making not a sound. I wait at attention, confused. After half a minute, I begin to turn my head to see him.

'*Moenie my loer nie, ek is nie 'n hoer nie!*' (Don't leer at me, I'm not a whore!) he snarls. He is immediately behind me, his voice low and intense.

I snap my eyes front. For perhaps four full minutes we stand there in the freezing night in absolute silence. My heart pounds with uncertainty; my senses are turgid with anticipation. I sense the rhythm of his breathing. I stare ahead at the tower, its stark silhouette piercing the winter constellations of the depthless night sky and I sense, too, his icy thrill of power.

Then he snaps suddenly, '*Voorwaarts mars!*' (Forward march!) and we march to the foot of the tower. I respond with the password to the guard's challenge and he emerges at the base. As I enter the rotund concrete belly of the tower I can hear the two marching back toward the guardhouse.

The shaft of the tower is musty and urinous. I mount the frozen iron ladder and pull myself up into the small round head of the tower, kicking the trapdoor into place behind me. I pull up the collar of my greatcoat; the tower is capped by a domed roof but is open on all sides and the night is achingly cold. The lieutenant and guard have disappeared. In the distance behind me security lights illuminate the grid of the camp, magazine, hangars, barracks. Below the tower, between high barbed wire fences, is the dog-run, with its central wire along which a bedraggled Alsatian drags its chain, trotting up and down, up and down, like a demented zoo animal, head down; tonight, though, it is huddled against the cold at the far end of the run. Beyond the fences a narrow cleared perimeter of earth is visible, then blackness, the vast barren blackness of the encircling scrubland and the impossible immensity of the night sky, tenuously linked on the eastern horizon by a dim seam of light where the tin roofs of the distant location shanties reflect the ancient glow of the stars.

For a couple of nights now the comet has been visible, traversing the eastern horizon, seemingly frozen in its interstellar ellipse. Perhaps it means something. But we have lost the sensibility for portents. I have watched it with a mixture of perplexity and melancholy from the tower these still, icy nights, a lonely body swinging across the universe on its doomed path, red tail flaring. There is little else to watch. The raking yellow beam of the searchlight reveals nothing, merely the sterile composure of the camp and the emptiness of the scrub. And everything is silent, except for the occasional monotone call of a nightbird, or the beat of a wing, or the chain's chink as the guard dog shakes itself. The field phone, if it works, has never rung.

And, but for the exhaustion and the cold, I am content here on the nightwatch, away from the mindless military routines, the training, inspection and parades, away from the numbing banalities of barrack chatter, the grating of Afrikaans, away from the inane necessities of all human contact. The monotony of the daywatch - staring out over the empty, uninhabitable wasteland - is blacked out. Alone in the tower amongst the stars I am restored to myself, staring deep into the profound nothingness. The constellations are distinct and bright, though I neither know their names nor understand their configurations. I recite poetry to myself, mainly Keats. I speak the gorgeous words out into the darkness - they are poems for the night - and they are reabsorbed into the universe, from where his soul, as Shelley says, beacons like a star. I know most of the odes by heart and am memorising the 'Ode to Psyche' tonight. The moonlight is not bright enough to read by, so I use my cigarette lighter, avoiding detection by placing my little pocket edition of the Complete Works on the floor, kneeling down, an acolyte, and shielding the light with my spreadeagled greatcoat. I have memorised all but the last verse by the time I hear the new guard approaching, unaccompanied, just before dawn. I challenge him, '*Gaan naai jou ma!*' (Go screw your mother!) he calls. I pick my book up and wipe a wet patch off the cover with my hand. It feels cold and slimy. Phlegm. That previous bastard. I wipe it again. My fingers are sticky. I rub them on my coat, lift the book to my nose: unmistakably, it is the primitive bleachy odour of semen.

Hints of grey have begun to taint the blackness; the dark hulks of the hangars assume a nebulous dissemblance. As I make my way across the vast tarmac, a sudden incandescent burst of light explodes on me from behind, hurling a startling black shadow a hundred yards ahead of me. It is so hallucinatory, the light, and that shadow so startling, springing from me like some dark emanation of myself, that I stop in my tracks, stunned, almost, as though awaiting the import of a revelation. Then I hear the familiar guffaw of the new guard who is arsing about with the searchlight. I walk on, without turning around, holding up a middle finger.

At the end of the transport section, I stop behind the last hangar and light a cigarette. This has been my final watch; I resume normal training today. After bungalow inspection we are to go on a full-pack route march. I watch the dawn gathering, igniting the horizon a sombre orange. The still air begins to thicken and weigh. It is going to be another scorching day. The moon, retreating down the yellowing sky, is a wraith-like shell of itself; the comet flares on with fading intensity.

As I stand there smoking, my eye is caught by a movement on the far side of the tarmac. It is a little black and white fox terrier, presumably belonging to one of the officers. It comes tripping across directly towards me, its nails clipping out a tattoo in the stillness. It does not bark, nor dance, nor sniff - it hardly even glances at me, simply comes and halts before me, as though for inspection. I squat down and stroke it. 'Hello, pups,' I say, 'hello.' It barely moves its little docked tail, just stands there, looking ahead, game legs firmly planted. I look; it is a bitch, I stroke her fine sleek head, scratch her head. The longer hair on her back is slightly coarse. I stroke and pat her, talking quietly, but she does not move or look at me at all. I stroke the firm little haunches, feeling their roundness. Between the back legs the hair is silky, the flesh soft. I run my fingers upwards, over the little hooded pudendum, with its whorl of hair. Then I gently insert my finger into the vagina. I had expected it to be small and tight, but my finger simply slips in. I am shocked to discover how wide, loose and facilitating the passage is. Such a small dog. And then the nauseating realisation descends, like a wet, suffocating sheet, upon me, that this dog is accustomed to such treatment - passively standing there, it accepts this abuse as affection - and I am filled with revulsion and self-disgust. To discover that others - smelly conscripts, pimply permanent-force corporals, officers, any of the inmates of this loathed place - have abused this dog as I have makes me burn with shame, as though I have, through this grossly levelling community of sin, myself been discovered.

I stand up and shoo the dog. She follows me a few paces, but I turn and stamp my boot and clap, and she trots off in a straight line across the tarmac.

———

The sun is at its fierce zenith as we finally reach the stifling summit of the hill, where we are permitted a smoke break, though we have to keep our packs on. We are exhausted, soaked through with perspiration, our khaki overalls blotched dark brown. There is no shade up here, no thorn trees nor aloes, just the baking iron boulders, where lizards gape, and the red, shard-strewn ground. The searing domes of our helmets cast small circles of shade round our boots. Each in his own little ring of shadow we stand in silent exhaustion, like animals. Below, the vast scrub-mottled valley ripples in the heat. When I get out of here, I think, when I get out … and stare down at the panorama. The camp, seven or eight miles distant, is clearly visible, the symmetrical grid of roads and buildings, parade grounds and towers, bounded by a hair-line perimeter of cleared earth, a futile laager surrounded by desolation. Miles to the east, in the next valley, the tree-lined oasis of Grahamstown, with its shimmering cathedral spire, its whitewashed university and old 1820 English Settler buildings, seems a vacuous mirage. Beyond that, on the furthest horizon, like the cryptic signals of a myriad mirrors, the tin roofs of the location shanties blaze. And it seems to me, standing here in my little corral of shade, that there is no getting out, that, encircled by sterility, there is only the movement from one barren circumscription to another. And I feel the thin corrosive poison of the place twisting in my veins.

Gringos, reggae gyals and 'le français de la souche recente'

Nation, diaspora and identity in football

Les Back, Tim Crabbe and John Solomos

The authors examine the significance of Jamaica's qualification for France 98.

Casablanca, 27 May 1998

Preparation for England's World Cup campaign reached a crucial stage as the team walked out for its 'warm up' match against Morocco in Casablanca. The fixture proved to be historic in ways that were not immediately apparent. The starting line-up included four black English players, which itself symbolised the profoundly multi-racial nature of the English professional game. It was also to mark the passing, although no one knew at the time, of a symbol of boozy English masculinity: it was to be Paul Gascoigne's last outing in an England shirt. With the teams lined up on the pitch, the stadium manager lost the tape with the recording of the English national anthem. A moment of silent chaos ensued.

Quickly the players, led by Ian Wright and captain Paul Ince, sang 'God Save the Queen' at the top of their voices and the travelling England fans - almost all of whom were white - joined in. The following day *The Sun* showed a picture of three black players, Ince, Wright and Sol Campbell, with Paul Gascoigne, depicted as national heroes singing their hearts out. The presence of black players in the England side has been an enduring feature of the national game since 1978 when Viv Anderson made his debut against Czechoslovakia. However, what has been striking recently is the number of black internationals playing the game at the highest level. But despite the presence of considerable numbers of black players in the England team comparatively few black fans actively support the national side.

Clearly, there are different things at stake when black and white people lay claim to icons of Englishness, or add their voice to the song of national stirring in sport. Paul Gilroy, perhaps more than anyone else, has pointed to the difference made when black people identify with Englishness and/or Britishness and in so doing establish new possible vectors of contingent racial inclusion.[1] This is a phenomenon common to European states with colonial histories that brought citizens from the colonial margin to the metropolitan centre through pre-established imperial networks and routeways. The sentiment embodied in the English fans' football song -'There ain't no black in the Union Jack - send the bastards back' - is a stark reminder of the intense articulation of race and nation. This is the context in which struggles over the possibility of 'black' and 'English/British' being repositioned in a relationship of inclusive mutuality takes on a political resonance. The situation in the United States is very different because these struggles over national belonging took on a very different form, where white supremacy has endured in a situation where people of colour are awarded the status of being 'American' without ambiguity.

Equally, black identifications with Englishness are not necessarily viewed as transformative. This is where the elision between notions of Englishness and Britishness becomes most acutely significant. During the game between England and Argentina which resulted in England's exit from the tournament by the inevitable penalty shoot out, Ian Wright, who missed the finals because of injury,

---

1. Paul Gilroy, *Small Acts: thoughts on the politics of black cultures*, Serpents Tail, 1993.

was pictured on UK television wrapped in a St George Cross flag. Lez Henry - a black fan - commented in the aftermath of the game:

> I looked at him [Wright] on the screen and I thought 'What the fuck is he doing - has he lost his mind completely!' I mean the St George Cross! That's the worst thing for a black person because according to them people you can't be black and English. Maybe Britishness would be something else because you can be 'black British' but English? Never.

The notion 'British' is widely held to be less racially or culturally exclusive and such identification can be sustained alongside associations with the Caribbean and the African diaspora.

Sport is a ritual activity in which the relationship between race, nation and inclusion is repeatedly stated and defined, through representations of the 'us' that is manifest between the team and its devoted supporters. Here, 'race' and 'nation' function not as given entities but social forms that are staged through 'big games' and repeated sporting dramas. Their form and quality are defined through the performance itself and continuities are established through repetition. So, here 'race' is not a given but the process in which 'racial difference' is invoked and connected with issues of identity, entitlement and belonging. Through focusing on the iterative dimension of these processes in sport, it is possible to identify moments in which ruptures occur which may challenge the tenets of racially exclusive nationalisms.

The relationship between these identity registers was brought into sharp focus through the Jamaican national team's debut at the World Cup finals in France 98. This article focuses on the ways in which nationhood was manifest around football during the tournament. It will look at the significance of the qualification of the Jamaican national team for the World Cup and the experience of Jamaican fans - many of whom were born in Britain - and the inclusion and identification embodied around the Jamaican team. The reason why we have focused on the Reggae Boyz is that something new seemed to be established by their supporters which stood in sharp contrast to the nature of English football and its associated supporter cultures. Here we want to look at the ways in which football provided a means through which nation and belonging was registered both 'at home' in the Caribbean and within the diaspora. The article concludes by looking at how this experience compared to the triumphant French national side who themselves seemed to embody a more 'racially diverse' representation of French nationhood. First, we want to plot the rise of the Jamaican team and its support.

'Reggae Boyz, Reggae Boyz, Reggae Boyz!': blackness, diaspora and the Jamaican national team

No-one really knows how the Jamaican team came to be named the 'Reggae Boyz'. The Jamaican Football Federation acted quickly and in March 1998 they registered 'Reggae Boyz' as a trademark in eleven countries. The official story is that the Zambians coined the name during a Jamaican national team tour in 1995, but in large part the name has stuck because of the pre-match concerts' fused football and dance-hall culture, where reggae stars like Dennis Brown and Jimmy Cliff performed. The road to the World Cup finals for Jamaica was followed keenly within the diaspora. This was made possible by global communications technology often associated with nascent European techno-imperialism. In south London a small pub called, ironically, *The Union Tavern* was the place where a packed house of black fans saw their team draw 0-0 with Mexico and earn their trip to Europe. These events in Kingston, Jamaica, had a distinctly local resonance given that this part of the metropolis has such a long standing Afro-Caribbean and specifically Jamaican community.

Elsewhere in London black fans watched the game on Sky Sports amid a carnival atmosphere. Alister Morgan, writing in *The Independent* (18/11/97, p31), told of the scenes at York Hall in East London where the game was watched by two thousand Jamaicans. One of the revellers told him:

It's not just a question of that round ball and 22 men. We're talking about the position of Jamaica and the efforts of a poor people. It's beyond football - in this country we live four and a half thousand miles from home and have been suffering for 40 years. Now Jamaica have qualified all Jamaicans will be uplifted.

This event provided a means for people within the diaspora to identify with Jamaica but it also offered black football fans a possibility to participate in football on their own terms. Equally, in the Caribbean Jamaica's qualification generated something of a partial process of national healing. Black music journalist John Masouri summed this up:

> Everyone I've spoken to remarks upon how a new sense of togetherness has swept the country since the team qualified for France ... the Reggae Boyz success has helped heal a fractured nation by instilling hope for a better future amongst their supporters. Crime rates have dropped and patriotism is back on the agenda, with the black, green and gold flag of Jamaica now to be seen fluttering everywhere. Even many Rastas are beginning to glow with a little nationalistic pride these days...[2]

Football provided a means both for domestic renewal and to re-animate connections within the diaspora.

The Jamaican team - coached by the Brazilian Rene Simoes - itself featured 'English' black players like Deon Burton of Derby County, Wimbledon's Robbie Earle and Paul Hall and Fitzroy Simpson, both of Portsmouth. The inclusion of players 'from foreign' caused some initial disquiet in Jamaica, where the *Daily Observer* (17/3/98) ran an article with the headline - 'No, we won't cheer for a team of British rejects'. Despite some disquiet in the Jamaican press, Horace Burrell, head of the Jamaican Football Association, was keen to assert the rights of any member of the diaspora to claim Jamaican heritage. In response to questions about the 'English contingent', he told John Masouri:

> Well, first of all let me correct you. It's not English players. They are Jamaican players whose parents came here [England] or they were born here, but we still regard them as Jamaicans. Our aim is to parade on the playing field in France the best 11 Jamaican players. That is our aim, and whether they live in England, Italy, the United States or Jamaica, if they've been able to parade the skills in the way Rene Simoes wants, then certainly they will be a member of the team (p13).

For Burrell an inclusive diasporic sensibility made perfect footballing and

---

2. John Masouri, 'Funkin for Jamaica,' *Echoes*, 13 June 1998, p12.

commercial sense.

As part of their pre-tournament preparation the Reggae Boyz played a series of friendly games in England. The first was a testimonial for the journeyman white player Simon Barker at Queen's Park Rangers on 22 March 1998. Unprecedented numbers of black people attended the game. Of the 17,000 fans packed into the stadium on that sunny Sunday afternoon probably all but a few hundred were black. Paul Eubanks, a journalist for the Caribbean newspaper *The Gleaner* (1/4/1998), wrote:

> Never ... had I seen so many black people inside one [football] ground.
> Generations of Jamaicans had come to watch the game. The most emotional
> moment for me was witnessing grandmothers at a site they would have never
> dreamed of entering, but they were getting ready to support their beloved
> team. The weather was consistent with its surroundings of Jamaicans: steel
> band and reggae music blaring out of the PA system, Jamaican patties on sale
> and even the odd 'funny' cigarette being passively smoked.

The significance of this event is hard to overstate. It marked not only the emergence of unprecedented numbers of black fans actively going to watch live football but also a shift in the nature of supporter culture. What this event revealed was the ethnocentrism of English football and its class-inflected and gendered nature. One of the striking things about the culture of Jamaican support was the transposition of the rituals associated with Jamaican musical cultures to the footballing context. There should be no surprise in this given the level of fanaticism about football both in the Caribbean and in London's black communities. English Premier league football is followed closely in Jamaica given the prominence of figures like John Barnes during his career at Liverpool and also Ian Wright at Arsenal. Football matters are debated each Saturday over the counter at virtually every black music record shop in Britain and in Britain there are plenty of football fans inside reggae music business itself. Earl Bailey and Nazma Muller, commenting on the long association between football and music in Jamaica, particularly in relation to Bob Marley, conclude:

> Every DJ worth his salt knows how to kick a ball ... Given the chance to
> marry both Jamaican loves, many entertainers turned up at the National

Stadium and away matches to rally fans behind the Reggae Boyz. From Beenie Man to Bounty Killer, Yellowman to Jimmy Cliff, they came out to support the national team.[3]

In the aftermath of qualification the reggae music industry set about the task of creating a theme tune for its footballing success. The first Reggae Boyz tune was recorded by the London reggae band The Black Astronauts, although this record was not widely distributed. Jamaica Unlimited's *Rise Up*, featuring Toots Hibbert, Diana King, Ziggy Marley and Maxi Priest was the official Reggae Boyz anthem. One of the best tunes, *Kick It*, was actually recorded by members of the team and released under the name Reggae Boyz. *Kick It* featured DJing from Donald Stewart - himself a musician - and vocals from Paul Hall and Fitzroy Simpson, over the Willie Williams' Studio One classic rhythm *Armagideon Time*. The tune has the distinction of being perhaps the only truly plausible pop record ever to be recorded by footballers. A flood of releases followed and singers and DJs gave lyrical tributes at live shows between November 1997 and the World Cup finals, be it at high profile concerts or sound-systems strung up in Kingston, New York or Birmingham.

The fusion of music and football garnered around the Jamaican team meant that the experience of going to games was quite unlike anything experienced in Britain before. John Masouri reflected in *Echoes* on the carnival atmosphere and sense of togetherness found in the English grounds where Jamaica played: 'many of us had never experience such warm, friendly vibes at football matches before'.[4] Football was also being opened publicly to black women in ways that were - in Britain at least - unprecedented. Plenty of black women had followed football privately and from afar but here they were watching football live. Marlene, a young woman born in London of Jamaican parentage, commented on her visit to Loftus Road:

It was good to go to football. I've never been to a game before but it wasn't really like the football you see on the TV, *it was just like going to a dance with*

---

3. Earl Bailey and Nazma Muller, *Jamaica's Reggae Boys: World Cup 1998*, Ian Randle Publishers and Creative Communications Inc, 1988, p88.
4. See note 2.

the music and everything. It was funny because I think the QPR players were a bit confused when they came out and saw all us black people and so few white faces in the crowd [my emphasis].

The participation of black women in football showed parallels with some of the broader patterns of female expression in Jamaican popular culture. In the context of the reggae dance-hall women have used music to engender female power through dancing and 'extravagant display of flashy jewellery, expensive clothes, elaborate hairstyles'.[5] Carolyn Cooper has argued that these performances embody complex gender politics in which women's power lies in the control over their own bodies and sexuality. Through dance-hall culture women have achieved high levels of autonomy and self-affirmation. Equally, their presence within football grounds has raised parallel issues with regard to those discussed previously in connection with the construction of black men within white masculinities in football. Here, black men can be respected through shared masculine codes but also viewed as being the bearers of racialised projections around issues of violence and sexuality. Clear traces of dance-hall culture are present amongst Jamaican football fans both in terms of their style and the significant numbers of young women in attendance at games.

The second game arranged for Jamaica in the UK was at Ninian Park against the Welsh national team on 26 March 1998. Paul, a black south London entrepreneur, had bought 1000 tickets and organised a fleet of 11 coaches to ferry the London Reggae Boyz and Reggae Gyals to the match from the capital. 'I want to give people a whole experience. You can get a coach to the game and then stay in Cardiff for an "after-party" reggae dance', he told me over the phone as I booked my ticket.[6] Midday outside Brixton Town Hall was an extraordinary sight as hundreds of black people assembled to make the long trip to Cardiff under the grey London skies. One man was dressed head to foot in black, green and gold like a walking Jamaican flag. Another was draped in a flag with a picture of Bob Marley in the centre and embroidered beneath

---

5. Carolyn Cooper, *Noises in the Blood: Orality, Gender and the 'Vulgar' Body of Jamaican Popular Culture*, Macmillan Caribbean, 1993, p155.
6. Although this paper is the result of a collective project, Les Back is the ethnographic interlocutor and these encounters within football culture are from the position of a white researcher.

the word 'Freedom'. Two young black women boarded the coach dressed in full Reggae Gyal style. One wore a green wig with a Jamaican team shirt and yellow pants, while her friend had a Jamaican flag coloured into her hair, wore a Jamaica scarf around her neck and a yellow and green leisure suit.

Sitting in front of me was a young woman call Pam. She was seventeen and had come to the game on her own, something that would be unthinkable under any other circumstances. An evening game at Ninian Park - home of Cardiff City - is a daunting place to visit even for the most seasoned football fan. Pam - who lives in Brixton - said:

> Well, I knew that I'd feel safe because I am travelling with all Jamaican people. It might be very different if it was another match. I like football but the first time that I have been to a game was when Jamaican played at Queens Park Rangers. I really liked it so here I am, and I get to go to a dance as well and I don't have to go to work tomorrow - do you know what I mean!

The whole experience of travelling with the Jamaican fans was so different from the usual football excursions to away games. Buju Banton and Beenie Man was played over and over on the sound system, fried chicken and bun was served as we sped down the motorway. But this contrast was more profound than just the quality of the music and the food on offer. The whole social basis of Jamaican fandom was much less tightly scripted than its English counterpart. Older women and men travelled with young people, fans travelled alone safe in the knowledge that they would be amongst their own. Black people who would not ordinarily step inside a football ground attended with the confidence of veterans.

The reality of the game against Wales was dismal in footballing and supporting terms: the game was an uneventful 0-0 draw. By the time that the coach arrived the rain was pelting down. The largest section of Jamaican support was located in the away stand which had no roof. The Jamaican performance was poor to say the least, but there was something inspiring in the fact that here were over five thousand black fans braving the wind and rain to watch their team. Behind me a black man in his sixties shouted 'Come on, Reggae Boyz'. The ball ricocheted off Ricardo 'Bibi' Gardener's shin, going out of play and ending another aimless run at the Welsh defence. He said, in a voice that was half growl and half whispered: 'The man play like cabbage'. This was a turn of phrase that I'd never heard inside a British football ground before but somehow it captured the moment perfectly. On the one hand this small comment registered a new presence, black people coming to football on their own terms with their own unique way of voicing frustration. On the other, it was the all too familiar *crie de coeur* of a disappointed fan, a phenomenon universal to people who share a passion for the game the world over.

So much nonsense has been written about the apparent unwillingness of black fans to attend English football matches, particularly in the case of the 1998 Football Task Force (FTF) report to the Ministry of Sport.[7] The reasons offered vary, from the out-and-out racist to claims about 'extenuating cultural and economic factors': 'black people don't watch football they follow basketball … they don't like to have to stand out in the cold … they can't afford to pay the high ticket prices'. Looking out on the legion of Jamaican fans that night in Cardiff, draped in black, gold and green with the rain trickling down their necks it became all too clear. The reason why they were here in these terrible conditions was because they felt this to be *their* team and *their* game. As the mass of black fans looked out onto Ninian Park and the Jamaican team, on this cold wet night, they saw themselves. The experience of English racism and the racially de-barred nature of British spectator sports is what prohibits an equal commitment and emotional bind being established between black fans and the England team and local clubs. This is true despite the fact that black players are playing at all levels of English football. One of the biggest cheers of the night was at half time when it was announced that England were losing 1-0 at Wembley.

'Gringos and dancehall queens': Parc des Princes, 21 June 1998

The setting was altogether different three months later at a sun drenched *Parc des Princes*, the occasion of Jamaica's second fixture of the finals against Argentina. The stadium was a patchwork of Jamaican gold shirts alongside the pale blue and white stripes of Argentina. Jamaican fans of all ages and of both sexes alongside pockets of Argentinian fans. The atmosphere was heavy

---

7. Football Task Force, *Eliminating Racism from Football: A Report by the Football Task Force submitted to the Minister for Sport*, The Football Trust, 1998, p28.

Paula and Debbie at
Parc des Princes

with anticipation. Two young female Jamaican fans dressed in classic dancehall queen style held court for the cameramen at the front of the stand. Later after the match the two women told me that they'd grown up in America: 'But we're Jamaican! Our parents came to New York from the Caribbean' said Debbie, who had her hair bleached and styled up in a kind of bouffant on top of her head. She wore a green leather top with green and yellow hot pants and big platform boots and one of her eyebrows was pieced with a silver ring. Her friend - Paula - was equally striking in her dance-hall style, her hair was permed and ironed so that it was straight up with red sunglasses resting on the top.

'It's been incredible coming to Europe to see the football. We've met so many Jamaicans in Paris and before that we stayed in London but here we are thousands of miles from Jamaica and it's like a big family reunion', she said after the game.

These two female fans were probably the most photographed women in Paris that day. Relentless waves of Argentinian and later Jamaican men had their photographs taken with them. One portly Argentinian wearing a national team shirt, a false moustache and a kind of wide brimmed gringo hat, posed with Debbie and Paula to the delight of the hordes of paparazzi. On the pitch there must have been a hundred photographers in an arc around this spectacle. An important question here is the degree to which these gendered performances are being re-inscribed as the pack of press photographers focused their lens. And, equally, how are these women being viewed by the male football fans who flocked to have their pictures taken with them? Sexual carnivalesque is part of the transgressive power of these styles of black femininity and the football stadium provided a new arena for their exposition. But part of Paula's and Debbie's allure - so evident amongst the Argentinian and other European men - may have been informed by dubious ideas relating to black women's sexuality and racial biology. Here, the transgressive potential of the dance-hall queen performance may in turn be re-inscribed by a male footballing audience which reduces these women and their agency to mere sex objects. The other danger of focusing too much on the dance-hall queens is that the substantial numbers of black women of all ages in the stadium are eclipsed because they followed the Jamaican team in a less stylised way.

The period before kick-off was charged with anticipation. This reached a kind of fever pitch about ten minutes before the start of the game when the guitar lick from the opening bars of Bob Marley's *Could You Be Loved* struck up on the stadium sound system. The whole place erupted with Argentinian and Jamaican fans alike singing and dancing. In an attempt to find a suitably 'Latin' equivalent to Bob Marley the French stadium manager immediately followed the reggae rhythm with 'La Bamba'. The choice of the Los Lobos version was somewhat ironic, given that this tune is a Mexican folk song, made famous in the 1950s by the Mexican-American rock'n'roll singer Richie Valens! Regardless, the packed stadium swayed, danced and sang together with equal intensity.

The game itself became almost a side issue as Jamaica slipped to a 5–0 defeat.

Martin Thorpe wrote in *The Guardian* (22/6/98) of the Jamaican side 'for all the infectious joy of their singing and dancing fans, the team simply could not match the high standards demanded on the global stage'. The Jamaican team were certainly treated like second-class citizens in the lead up to this fixture. Robbie Earle recounted the shoddy treatment that they received from the FIFA officials - the team's pre-game warm up on the pitch was shortened to suit the Argentinians, and they were ushered away despite Simoes's objections so that the ground could be prepared for the corporate spectacle (*Observer*, 28/6/98).

> Incidents like these highlight the fact that we are not yet looked upon as equal. FIFA have based much of their promotion on fair play - it is time that they applied it across the board. Is it not the mentality of a bully to identify its weaker targets and pick on them? We have enough work to do on our own to climb the soccer ladder without any obstructions from the game's administrators.

Maybe the Jamaican team were out of their depth on the field, but something significant had definitely happened within the stadium itself. There had been a

Outside the Parc des Princes

transformation in the *Parc des Princes* - the ground which is home to Paris St Germain, a team with a reputation for a racist following amongst its fans. A black friend who'd lived in Paris told of an experience watching Liverpool FC there in the European cup in 1996: 'It was an incredible atmosphere and the racism was very open. It was funny in a way because we were standing with the Paris St Germain fans and one of the skinheads came up to me and advised me to go and stand somewhere else for my own safety!'

At half time, and along with a stream of Argentinian and Jamaican fans, I made for the toilets. Descending down a long staircase, bordered by grim grey concrete walls, this throng of supporters were confronted with the inscriptions of hate which laid claim to the ground and registered its history. Racist graffiti were plastered over virtually every surface of the toilet area. Above the sinks where a black man was washing his son's hands was the inscription 'SKINHEADS' alongside scribbled Celtic Crosses and Swastikas. Elsewhere, FN stickers with a flame coloured red, white and blue were plastered on the cubicles, 'SS's and Swastikas scratched into the surface of the metal doors. The fans seemed to ignore these graphic racist outpourings. As I watched the little boy's hands being washed, I noticed the Jamaican motto on the back of his gold and green shirt: 'Out of many, one goal!' Here a multi-cultural footballing reality was confronted with the subterranean traces of racist football culture. Turning to leave I looked up, and daubed in English on the open door was the slogan 'WHITE POWER'. Ascending the stairs this image was etched on my mind and provided a stark warning that the transformations manifest around this fixture and the considerable numbers of black fans present was both a temporary and conditional phenomenon.

Jamaican support during France 98 provided a pretext for the diaspora to gather in one place. What was striking was that people of Jamaican descent had converged on Paris from a range of itinerant homes, be they in New York, London, Manchester or Birmingham. Also striking was the range of backgrounds that Jamaican fans demonstrated, in terms of age group, gender and class background. As we boarded the bus for the long drive back Calais and then via the channel tunnel to London, a man in his late forties sat down next to me. He hadn't been part of the outward journey which had been something of a party. The scene after the match was altogether more subdued. The man sitting next to me seemed dejected from the 5-0 trouncing. He appeared a little remote and aloof and just sat there making no gestures towards conversation, wearing a Jamaican team shirt, with a beaten up full size football on his lap. Occasionally, he'd lift his Jamaican team, baseball cap off his head, then tug it down firmly and then rub his eyes.

After about an hour and a half, we started to talk. My travelling companion's outwardly aloof appearance was for good reason. To my surprise he told me that he was one of Jamaica's eighteen High Court judges! He lived outside Kingston and he'd travelled to France to see the World Cup with a package deal, taking the opportunity to see Europe, including Belgium, Luxembourg and Amsterdam. I told him that I couldn't imagine an English judge going to France to watch England play. 'Well they think of me as a bit of a radical back at home' he said. I asked him how many people had made the trip to from Jamaica to France. 'Quite a few, quite a few', he replied. 'Probably about 5-600 and that's quite a lot when you consider what a small island Jamaica is compared to European countries.' Here I was sitting discussing everything from sport to sociology with a High Court judge in a football shirt! The remarkable diversity found amongst Jamaican football fans seemed to be epitomised in this one unexpected moment.

'Noir, blanc et bleu?': France 98, nationalism and the return of Roland Barthes

In an increasingly globalised world, sporting spectacles like the World Cup offer one of the last vestiges in which nationalism can be expressed ritually and celebrated. The sportswear companies, media corporations and merchandising moguls set out their wares too, all vying for a piece of this festival of corporate multi-culturalism. It seemed apt that the final itself, between Brazil and France, was also the stage of a confrontation between the finalists' respective sponsors, sportswear moguls Nike and Adidas. Even before a ball was kicked Nike edged its superiority in the product placement stakes. Nike overtook Adidas in the *Financial Times* World Cup sponsors index (11/7/98), which measured brand exposure through the teams wearing the various companies' kit.

France 98 provided the ultimate stage for the 'world game' and the world was watching as the host nation triumphed. But something else beyond corporate fortunes was also at stake that merits serious attention. What makes football interesting is that it provides one of the few spheres in which ideas about identity, ethnicity and race can be expressed, embodied and performed. It offers the possibility for nationhood to be represented through, either: a grotesque pageant of fixed archetypes; or, as a carnival in which the circumscriptions of the national body politic - particularly in terms of race - can be breached, even partially dissolved, giving life to new possibilities.

The potential of national sport to possess a recombinant potential was particularly relevant in the aftermath of the French victory. Two years prior to *la Coupe Du Monde*, National Front leader Jean Marie Le Pen had famously rebuked the French team - particularly those whose family origins lay outside of France - for their lack of zeal when singing the Marseillaise. Arguing against such multi-ethnic presences, he said: 'It's unnecessary to bring players in from abroad and baptise them as the French team.' The French national team displayed an incredible diversity and many of its stars were born outside of metropolitan France, including the Ghanaian Marcel Desailly, Christian Karambeu from New Caledonia, Senegal's Patrick Viera, and Lilian Thuram of Guadeloupe. Still others would qualify as what Le Pen would call *Français de souche recente*, meaning that such players were not 'real Frenchmen' because their parents were too recent migrants. These would include Alain Boghossian (Armenia), Vincent Candela (Italy), Bernard Diomende (Guadeloupe), Youri Djorkaeff (former Yugoslavia), Thierry Henry (Guadeloupe), and the goal scoring hero of the victory over Brazil, Zinedine Zidane (Algeria).

The victory itself seemed immediately to be a triumph over Le Pen's version of racially exclusive nationalism. Philippe Jérôme wrote, 'Zidane's two goals in the World Cup final did more for the equal rights of citizens than a thousand speeches from the left denouncing racism and the policies of Jean-Marie Le Pen's National Front' (*Guardian* G2, 15/7/98).

Jérôme was not alone in claiming the victory marked the arrival of a multi-racial French nation. A host of people from the pantheon of French cultural and academic celebrities lauded the triumph as a moment of imminent togetherness. This included people as diverse as film stars and musicians like Catherine Deneuve, Gerard Depardieu and Johnny Hallyday, and the likes of Isabelle Huppert and Jacques Chirac. Nick Fraser wrote of an incident he overheard near the Hôtel de Ville in which an elderly white French woman said gratefully to two Arab girls: 'If we win it will be because of you ... we should have had blacks and Arabs in the team earlier. If we had done we would have won more matches' (*Guardian* G2, 15/7/98). Equally, it would be wrong to dismiss the presence of Arabs and black citizens among the celebrating crowds, given that the French have suburbanised urban poverty and confined their immigrant populations to the desolate *banlieues* that circle Paris. The visual presence on the Champs Elysées of these otherwise urban outcasts was significant in that it registered their presence in the national imagination in a less pathological way.

In the aftermath of the French victory one could almost sense the excitement of cultural critics on the left as the pages of the liberal press turned and quivered each morning in Paris and London. However, such new found enthusiasm runs perilously close to a kind of trite Zeitgeist hermeneutics, a syndrome which cultural studies - especially that inspired by literary criticism - has sometimes suffered from. One detail quickly dismissed was Le Pen's response: 'I claim this victory for the National Front who designed its framework'. Le Pen's apparent change of tack was thought by many to be evidence of a deceitful and fickle opportunism. But perhaps this apparent change of heart is not as complete as it might seem, and Le Pen's views need not necessarily be in direct opposition to the nascent celebration of French diversity in sport. Le Pen argued that France could be 'composed of different races and religions' so long as they were French first and foremost. Such a discussion recalls the observations of another famous Frenchman, Roland Barthes.

In *Mythologies*, Barthes's classic study in semiology, he recounts being handed a copy of *Paris Match* in a barber shop:

> On the cover, a young Negro in a French uniform is saluting, with his eyes uplifted, probably fixed on a fold of the tricolour. All this is the meaning of the picture. But, whether naively or not, I see very well what it signifies to me: that France is a great empire, that all her sons, without colour discrimination, faithfully serve under her flag, and that there is no better answer to the detractors of an alleged colonialism than the zeal shown by this Negro in serving his so-called oppressors.[8]

The connection here between the black French soldier and black athletes recalls Norbert Elias's famous discussion of the 'civilising process', and the key role that

---

8. Roland Barthes, *Mythologies*, Paladin Books, 1973, p116.

sport has played in what he referred to as the internal pacification of Western societies.[9] But here sport might play a significant role in the transition from colonial to postcolonial government. In fact, one might read the fervour generated over the multi-racial French national team as the return - albeit in a neo-colonial form - of a Barthian myth.

F or Barthes, a mythical concept derives its power not from didacticism or propaganda, but rather from its ability to naturalise what is essentially an ideological relation. It is through such an embodied implicitness that its mythic definitions work. So, the picture of the Negro soldier saluting the Tricolour conjures the concept of French imperiality without naming it, or announcing its arrival. Rather, it is presented as a natural state, 'as if the signifier *gave foundation* to the signified' (*Mythologies*, p13). Similarly we might think of the spectacle of a multi-racial French team as the embodiment of a mythical concept. 'For no man or woman really believed in a multi-cultural France', wrote Nick Fraser (*Guardian* G2, 15/7/98). 'They left what they considered to be considered to be a grotesque illusion to Americans, British and Dutch ... French people probably merely wanted foreigners to be *more like themselves*' [emphasis added]. The French version of diversity amounts to little more than an assimilationist nationalism that insists on a sovereign French identity above all else. It is perhaps not surprising that its new hero, Zinedine 'Zizou' Zidane, is the son of an Algerian soldier - a 'harki' - who came to France after fighting alongside the colonialists *in opposition* to Algerian independence. Multi-racial France - as a mythical concept - embodies within the theatre of national sport complex combinations of national transcendence and neo-colonial accommodation.

In this article we have explored the relationship between nation and race in contrasting European settings and in a diaspora community. Jamaican fans utilised a rhetoric of nationhood that confounded any simple notion of its borders. This provided a stark contrast to assimilating European nationalisms for whom visas of entry for black citizens are only issued with specific terms and conditions. The support garnered by the Jamaican national team from black metropolitan communities shows the vital and animate resonance of Caribbean

---

9. Norbert Elias and Eric Dunning, *The Quest for Excitement: Sports and Leisure in the Civilising Process*, Blackwell 1969.

belonging within the diaspora in Europe. The itinerant belonging to England - often challenged by popular racism both in football and outside - co-existed with a strong commitment to the vibrant diasporic registers of Jamaican football. Football momentarily gave a glimpse of unity to this fractured Caribbean nation, best expressed in the utopian tones of reggae music. Tony Rebel chants these telling lines in Jamaica Unlimited's *Rise Up*:

> Because of you.
> Progress.
> I have seen oneness and difference in this country.
> Don't be intimidated, even when tested.
> Small axe can fell a big tree.

The significance of football as a form of popular culture is in the identifications and definitions it allows to be articulated and defined ritually. This is expressed in the space that lies between the fan collective and their team's iconic status. It is important to look at this encounter, for it is where the micro-politics of race, nation and belonging are lived.

The paper is part of a wider project entitled The Cultures of Racism in Football *which was funded by the Economic and Social Research Council. We would like the thank the ESRC for their support. Thanks to Michael Keith for his critical comments and John Masouri for sharing his unique insight into the connection between reggae music and football. Also, thanks to Colin King, Sharon Davidson, Lez Henry, Garry Robson, Ben Gidley and John Curran. This work is drawn from a book that will published by Berg in 1999 entitled* The changing face of football: racism, multiculture and identity in the English game.

Reading the signs

Christine Clegg

Gordon Burn, *Happy Like Murderers*, Faber and Faber, £17.99

Among other things, Gordon Burn has a gift for ventriloquism. The ability to catch and replay the speech patterns and texture of the language of his subjects is something that sets his books about murderers apart from the rest of the 'true crime' genre. But even while he is respected for the thoroughness of his research - the scrupulous checking of facts and information - his willingness to move in so closely raises troubling questions about identification. In his earlier book, *Somebody's Husband, Somebody's Son: The Story of Peter Sutcliffe* (Mandarin 1984), Burn's ear for the language of John Sutcliffe, the father of Peter Sutcliffe, sometimes makes it difficult to see quite where Burn stands. Nicole Ward Jouve, in her analysis of the Sutcliffe case ('*The Streetcleaner': The Yorkshire Ripper Case on Trial*, Marion Boyars, 1986), observes that Burn's ... 'unquestioning use of John Sutcliffe's own language makes him sound like an "adoptive son"'. That same grasp of spoken language (this time, the hybrid dialect of urban and rural Gloucestershire) is powerfully present in Burn's new book about Fred and Rose West, *Happy Like Murderers*. But there is never any question here about where Burn stands, especially in relation to Fred West. In conjunction with the cadences of the spoken lives, the narrative forcefully articulates the sense of a 'moral void' at the 'heart' of the Wests. More than just mapping out an absence, though, Burn finds a way of dwelling inside the terrible home ground of the Wests, and at the same time speaking from an ethical position.

Nevertheless, the question of authorial identification remains fraught because it risks installing readers in the lived psychodrama of the Wests. This fear of coming too close to a degraded reality has always been one of the major difficulties with the West case, ever since the news of the horrible discoveries at 25 Cromwell Street appeared in 1994. On the one hand, the newspapers appeared to be saturated with coverage of the story throughout the digging up of evidence in the form of human remains, the suicide of Fred West, the eventual trial and conviction of Rose West, and, finally, the release of biographical details about the young women who were abducted, tortured, murdered and mutilated. But it was equally obvious, both from the reluctance of the BBC to reveal some of the evidence given in the trial (as being too horrible to hear), and from the absence of serious analysis in the quality press, that there was something unmanageable about the Wests and their crimes. The media representation of Rose West, and the rhetoric of perverse femininity which, not surprisingly, linked her with Myra Hindley, gave rise to discussions in feminist publications about the idea of female serial killers. The usual charges of sensationalism against the media were oddly misplaced, though, because the crimes were so grotesquely excessive, and since the question of the extent of Rose West's culpability remains unresolved. Indeed, what Burn draws attention to is that it is virtually impossible to exaggerate the horror given that the Wests appear to have broken every taboo the law attempts to enshrine, including incest, child murder, and mutilation.

I n his review of *Happy Like Murderers* (*Guardian* 26.9.98), Andy Beckett describes Burn as 'the perfect coffee table ghoul'. Whilst appearing to cast doubt on the moral purpose of the book, Beckett concedes that it contains a 'moral core' - the careful registration of the neglect of the outside world in the face of the West's activities. I would agree that this is crucial to an understanding of Burn's mission. One of the central arguments of *Happy Like Murderers* turns on the failure of the 'outside world' to intervene. Moreover, this failure to act represents a cultural illiteracy - a failure of interpretation, an inability to read the conglomeration of signs and codes. Dope is a recurrent theme here, serving as a timely distraction both to the police, who were continually raiding the West house for drugs, and to the 'floaters and drifters', the stoned lodgers who were switched off to the violence and routine sexual brutality in the 'safe' house at the end of the urban hippy trail. Similarly, throughout the lengthy Yorkshire ripper investigations, the police were switched off, albeit for different reasons, to the remarkably obvious signs that linked Peter Sutcliffe with the sexual murders of women in the North of England between 1975 and 1981. They failed to read the evidence that stared up at them from the ground - the boot-print, the tyre-print. As Nicole Ward Jouve comments in her analysis of the case, the signs were 'there for all to see but invisible because so blatant'. It is such blatancy that marks the history of the Wests at every turn. Burn confronts us with the confusions about criminal templates - conscious and unconscious - that persist in culture. What does a criminal look like, act like? How can we tell where the harm will come from? Not everything is known about the West murders. But the connections between evidence of disappearances, abused children, pornography and prostitution, as well as the criminal records for rape, indecent assault, and actual bodily harm, added up to something significantly amiss in the West household.

T angential to the contemporary mood of sexual liberation, but not of it since liberation suggests resistance to prohibitions, every aspect of the West family life was sexualised. As children, both Fred and Rose experienced the sexualisation of everyday life in which the only imperative - the law handed down - was that father has his way. Fathers are *entitled* to sex with whoever they want. Not the incest taboo as the symbolic means of entry into culture, but incest as 'nature's way' of enforcing real father rights on children - 'Dads know how to do it right', Fred tells his children (p120). At the same time, and in contrast to the incestuous insularity, there is exchange with the world outside. Fred, as husband, and father, is willing to hand 'his women' over, on the provision that he gets to look and to listen. Since the primacy of the black man's penis is the object of Fred's desire through Rose, black men never have to pay for sex. Payment comes in the form of the 'donation' of semen to Rose which creates 'love children' and foments Fred's sexual potency. Burn exhaustively demonstrates that living out Fred's desires was a full-time job for Rose. Fred was also consumed by working on their home at Cromwell Street. The building, rebuilding, constructing, levelling, and reconstructing was continuous - a life project with no planning permissions. Fred West's home was a permanent building site - building for the sake of building, killing for the sake of killing. His fixation with bits and pieces of machinery, scrap, tools and junk, which in itself is already a perversion of benign means of making-do and mending, is discharged into the dead bodies of murdered girls and women, and engineers the sexual persecution of his children. Not just father's right to everyday sexual activity and torment, but father's right to rig up dirty old metal contraptions in and around the bodies of his living, breathing children.

If the anarchic hatred of authority and officialdom kept Fred West just outside the law - mostly, he got away with things - the Wests as 'family' were just about attached through the children to the social fabric of schools, hospitals, health visitors and so on. Retrospectively, it is easy to say that people should have known, should have acted, should have intervened, should have read the signs, but it is also fair to say that the kinds of institutional structures and practices that have been implemented in the wake of the scandals of Cleveland, for instance, were simply not in place at the time the Wests were operating. In this sense they are both symptom and evidence of the failure to protect children from bad parents, whether real or surrogate. There is, of course, the matter of Rose's sexual enslavement to Fred, but the question of her own desires remains complicated. Officially, Rose was a minor when she 'took up' with Fred. The children's enslavement is another matter. Burn gives due and proper emphasis to the murdered victims of the Wests, but he also, rightly, does justice to the terrible suffering of the West children who survived. They were continuously subjected to cruelties and deprivation in a pornographic atmosphere of sexualised activities, gestures and speech, in a place where everything came back to sex or death. Testament to this is the ritualised recording for posterity - the photographing, the cremating and, lastly, the bottling - of Rose's (black) semen stained black knickers.

For Andy Beckett, the Wests are, in the end, 'too unique'. Implicitly, this means that they are so exceptional, such a deviation, that we can learn nothing from them. Whilst Burn is scrupulous about not making bold claims, he resists the temptation to remove them from other ways of interpreting and understanding the cultures we inhabit. By introducing the book with a reconstruction of the life of Caroline Raine, the young woman who, uncannily, escaped twice from the Wests and eventually brought charges of indecent assault and actual bodily harm against them, Burn powerfully conveys the sense of the violent interruption to the lives of the young women who were murdered. The circular effect of the narrative works to emphasise the unfolding and escalating horror as figures disappear suddenly from the (textual) landscape. This circularity also cuts up and disperses the otherwise relentless pornography of the serial sexual violence of the Wests. But the stylistic device of reworking the same sentiment can start to feel like an intrusive repetition that the narrative could well do without.

If the figure of Caroline Raine comes to stand in for those others who cannot be represented, the patient exploration of her early life enables Burn to track the innumerable harms and cruelties, deliberate and circumstantial, that adults inflict on children. Caroline discovers years later, for instance, that her stepfather had intercepted all the cards, letters and small gifts of money sent to her by her real father when she moved with her mother to the Forest of Dean. This does not mean that we can, in a simplistic way, put the Wests at the extreme end of a continuum of family dysfunction and parental abuse; but neither can we obliterate them from the bounds of understanding, even if they were, in Beckett's words, 'beyond morals'.

Although *Happy Like Murderers* manages the difficult task of maintaining enough distance for the reader to approach the 'moral vacuum' of the Wests, the author's antipathy towards Fred West is palpable. In one sense it drives the narrative. For all Fred West's 'bullshitting' and ridiculous posturing, he *was* able to go about doing what he wanted to women and children, unimpeded by the laws to which most of human society is subject. And it is here that the ethical moment of the book can be precisely located, I think, in Burn's attempt - too late for the victims - to read the signs of dereliction in that bleak place where the cultural prohibitions - the laws of human society - failed so abysmally.

Slumbering in the lap of social labour

David Goldblatt

Lester R. Brown, Christopher Flavin and Hilary French (eds), *State of the World*, Earthscan, £12.95

Marx was right about the magnitude of the forces - both destructive and creative - unleashed by capitalism. Reading State of the World *has led David Goldblatt to reflect on the sheer scale of the environmental degradation this has led to.*

One hundred and fifty years after the publication of the Communist Manifesto it is clear to almost everyone that the old boy was wrong about almost everything. He was wrong about the environmental consequences of capitalism, and particularly wrong about the harmonious potential of socialism's relationship with the natural world.

But no wonder - Marx and the social changes he described were of their moment. And what a moment it was: after thousands of years of painfully slow economic development, the growth of capitalism seemed to mean that humanity was on the verge of escape.

The reality of agrarian societies had been widespread, grinding poverty. The fabulous wealth of ancient elites had been extracted from minuscule economies. Wretchedly poor peasantries had battled the vagaries of an unconquered and spiteful nature. The growth of pre-modern economies was always constrained by social forces and by natural limits. Now, at last, the unbridled energies and technologies of industrial capitalism would transcend the limits of agrarian economics. Fossil fuels and machines were replacing human and animal muscles as sources of energy and work. Inorganic materials were replacing scarce and depleted natural resources. Markets, capital and capitalists, unfettered by political and social restraints, would finally force the natural world to yield its potential riches.

Of course, the environmental consequences of this breakout were becoming apparent in the filth and smoke of the early industrial city. But, like the miserable poverty of the new working class, this was a mere problem of transition. With the inevitable arrival of socialism and the dissolution of the capitalist mode of production, poverty and pollution would be banished. As we know, it hasn't quite worked out that way.

Industrial capitalism has lifted perhaps one quarter of humanity out of poverty and raised them to dizzying heights of prosperity, while the rest of the planet continues to live either near, on, or beyond, the margins of survival. Nature has yielded its riches to some, but the degradation and pollution that Engels found in Manchester has proved far from transitional. In fact, the environmental consequences of capitalist development have multiplied in scope, scale, complexity and danger. As for the harmonious reunion of humanity and environment under socialism, it perished long ago in the toxic wastelands of Siberia and the macabre mutilated forests of Bohemia and Silesia.

Yet rereading the Communist Manifesto today one cannot but be struck by Marx's profound grasp of the elemental dynamism of capitalism. Marx's enduring relevance is that he combined an appreciation of the sheer quantitative expansion of capitalist economies with a lucid sense of their broader structural consequences: their unparalleled capacity to transform the most ancient and deeply embedded patterns of economic, political and social life; the terrifying, vertiginous velocity they impart to economic and social change. Marx, writing at a moment of glorious industrial take-off and ecological ignorance, may have been oblivious to the systemic toxic payback of the new mode of production, but he was in no doubt about the exponential increase it brought in humanity's collective power to transform the earth. In this respect Marx was, and is, particularly correct.

> The bourgeoisie, during its rule of scarce one hundred years, has created more massive and colossal productive forces than have all the preceding generations together. Subjection of nature's forces to man ... clearing of whole continents for cultivation, canalisation of rivers, whole populations conjured out of the ground - what earlier century had even a presentiment that such productive forces slumbered in the lap of social labour?

Had Engels a copy of *State of the World* to hand as he read over the manuscript, he might well have noted in the margin, 'You ain't seen nothing yet'.

On almost indicator you care to take - and *State of the World* has no shortage of them - the evidence is unambiguous. Forests are shrinking and deserts are expanding. Water tables are falling and greenhouse emissions are rising. Toxic and nuclear wastes accumulate in the environment, while soils are eroding. The planet is hotting up, the polar ice caps are fragile and species are being extinguished faster than we can count them. We are experiencing unprecedented levels of environmental degradation and there are no economic systems and ideologies left to blame, except for one.

Is this just another case of environmentalist crying wolf? After all the crude computer projections of doom produced by the Club of Rome in the 1970s have long since been discredited, and the relationship between economic and demographic growth and environmental degradation is not fixed. But, in the last twenty-five years, the profile of environmental degradation has been transformed. While the early depletionists worried about the exhaustion of fossil fuel supplies and local urban air pollution, we are now faced with the exhaustion of irreplaceable forest and global climatic change. The problem is not that we will be unable to find new oil deposits, but that we have burnt too much already. It may be that some Western economies have managed to squeeze a little more output from a little less raw material, and that the crudest indicators of air and water pollution have peaked in the West. But these benign developments have been swamped by the environmental consequences of two decades of explosive economic growth in East Asia and elsewhere in the developing world, and the recognition of a multiplicity of new forms of pollution and ecological stress: ozone depletion, global warming, etc. It is difficult not to conclude that, under current circumstances, the quantitative expansion of the global capitalist economy will lead to levels of natural resource loss and ecosystem disruption that will place constraints upon future economic development and pose threats to political stability, as great as those that were faced by the fragile agrarian societies of the pre-modern world. The closing numbers at the end of the twentieth century do not look good.

In 1850 the population of the planet had reached 1.2 billion people. There are now 5.8 billion of us and, although the exponential curve is beginning finally to flatten, there will be another 3.6 billion of us by 2050. In 1950 the crude value of global output stood at $5 trillion. Between 1990 and 1997 the global economy grew by another $5 trillion to stand at a total value of $29 trillion. In seven years we have managed to generate the same volume of growth as the entire human race managed from the emergence of the species until 1950. The mathematics of these of these growth rates is dizzying. Assuming an annual rate of global growth of only 4 per cent, output will more than double every twenty years. In 2050 the earth will be supporting 9.4 billion people and an economy whose annual production will be in the region of $200 trillion. How much of the world's ecosystem will make it to 2050, and in what condition, are other matters.

In the last century the world had already lost more than half of its original forest cover, mostly in Europe and North America. In the closing decades of the twentieth century the insatiable demand for lumber and paper in the West, and for export dollars, new land and firewood in the developing world, has seen a third of what is left disappear. Satellite imagery shows the steady retreat of forest from the urban sprawl of breakneck urbanisation. Reckless deforestation, by poor peasants, corrupt governments and their corporate cronies, has brought about species loss, soil erosion, flooding on a spectacular scale and uncontrollable raging fires. While more marginal land is cleared for crop production, more water is drawn from unsustainable aquifers and river courses to irrigate it. Every year the great Colorado, Ganges and Yellow rivers that irrigate the vast farmlands of the Southwestern USA, Northern India and Eastern China, run dry for longer and longer. Yet the planet's grain stocks are falling, prices are inching up, and the politics of food, land and water scarcity appear on the near horizon.

The world's fisheries are already on that horizon. A quadrupling of the global fish catch in the last fifty years has left eleven of the world's fifteen major fisheries on the point of collapse. The signs of economic desperation and ecological crisis are clear. 69 per cent of the world's major fish species are in serious decline. And the carbon capitalism of the West and its remorseless global duplication has produced a quadrupling of fossil fuel burning in the last fifty years, and an even greater increase in greenhouse gas emission. We are now experiencing the fastest rate of atmospheric change for 10,000 years. The American-Arabian petro-chemical complex may consider it mere coincidence that the thirteen warmest years since planetary records of temperature began have all occurred since 1979; nobody else seems to.

Can it be that even the most Promethean and optimistic observer does not find these raw figures daunting? Can they ignore the fact that the US economy is currently responsible for a quarter of an already unsustainable global level of greenhouse emissions? Can they honestly believe that a global population of 9.4 billion people, all aspiring to a standard of living set by American and Western consumers, is a plausible future?

I, for one, am daunted by these figures and prospects. But the questions that they raise are even more daunting: how is that environmental issues continue to occupy, at best, a small part of the political agenda, in even the most amenable political cultures? What can feasibly be done to bring the environmental appetite of the global economy within the pale of sustainability? And who will do so, and what are their chances? The unsettling consequence of reading *State of the World* is that it forces one to pose these questions without providing much help in answering them.

W hat is then that keeps these most pressing of issues at some remove from the centres of political energy and power? In the 'developing' world the answer is simple - poverty. It is poverty and the perverse incentive systems of unregulated capitalism that fuel the unsustainable consumption of precious natural resources and ecosystems, by individuals, governments and corporations. Authoritarian polities do not help matters, not least because they make it so hard for environmentalists and local peoples to organise and protest. But, as India demonstrates, democratic politics is no guarantee of sustainable economic development. In any case, it is unthinkable for politicians and publics alike, with so many people denied access to the most basic of essential goods and services, let alone a measure of Western affluence, that economic growth should be curtailed, whatever the environmental consequences. This will not wash in the West. Despite the persistence of relative poverty and social exclusion, we have already bloated ourselves on more than our fair share of resources, and poisoned ourselves and everybody else with more than our fair share of environmental problems. It is clear then, for reasons of both justice and realpolitik, that any meaningful response to global environmental problems must begin in the West.

Are there reasons for optimism? It could be argued that western economic development has created favourable conditions for the emergence of environmental politics. Affluence, security, liberal democracy and widespread higher education appear to be important preconditions for the emergence of contemporary environmental movements. One can overplay the argument that the environment is marginal in the public and political cultures of the West. Survey after survey reports people's desire for a cleaner environment and some willingness to pay for it. Membership of and donations to environmental NGOs are healthy. Corporate reports pay homage to environmental impact assessments and sustainable mission statements. From almost nowhere in the last thirty years every polity in the OECD has acquired a comprehensive body of environmental legislation, and enforcement agencies. While the progress of explicitly environmental parties has been, at best, limited, most mainstream political parties have been forced by public pressure to adopt environmental policies, however insincere or partial. These are important achievements. Yet when measured against the scale of the threats facing us, they appear insubstantial.

When it comes to the crunch, the greening of our political cultures and institutions evaporates. In no national election - with perhaps the exception of the Swedish debate over nuclear power - has the environment figured as the central concern of politicians or electorates. In no nation has an economic policy been elaborated or implemented, in government, in which the environmental consequences of unchecked economic growth has occupied more than a secondary status. In the major economies of the world this task has barely acquired any status at all. No project of international environmental concern or institution building has been graced with even a fraction of the political energy and resources devoted to the creation of an international free trading order, the creation of a single European currency, or the stabilisation of bankrupt financial systems and their authoritarian rulers.

P erhaps the most important reason that so little has been done is that the individual and collective consequences of turning unsustainable growth into sustainable development are so enormous. Paradoxically, the more clearly defined and reasoned the environmentalist response becomes - *and State of the World* provides just such a response - the more improbable its likely implementation appears. A global demographic, industrial and agricultural revolution must be combined with a vast global transfer of environmentally benign capital and technology from the West to the rest. All of this must be achieved in a time scale of perhaps half a century and it must be done against the current grain of pricing structures, subsidies, incentives, and profit opportunities around which the global economy currently spins.

Extraordinarily, the policy package that might initiate such a process is not entirely utopian. Global flows of capital and technology are already immense, while the influence of international environmental law and institutions is unprecedentedly large. It is not inconceivable that a global historical compromise could be negotiated between them; Western capital could be directed towards profitable but environmentally beneficial infrastructure development in the South; the terms of trade in international agricultural markets could be made to reflect the environmental costs of production. A range of energy and material efficient technologies exist that would, if widely distributed, make a considerable impact on the West's environmental appetite. If the World Bank diverted into diffusing these technologies and practices in the developing world a modicum of the time and energy which it currently devotes to funding environmentally disastrous dams and reclamation schemes, we might begin to pull back from the brink. An environmental overhaul of the currently insane taxation and subsidy system of advanced and developing capitalism would make a significant contribution to such a project. Imagine harnessing the inventive dynamism of the capitalist mode of production to these tasks.

Imagine too the electoral consequences of running on such a programme, and the political consequences of trying to implement it. As with any process of social change it is much clearer, prior to the process of transition, who will be losers than who will be the winners. An immediate roll-call of losers would include: the petro-chemical, energy and water industries; the car and road industries and their interminable retinue of add-on products and services; agribusiness and monster Fordist fisheries; firms and consumers dependent upon wasteful production and destructive consumption, like cheap processed foods, unnecessary packaging, tobacco, disposable products of all kinds; company profits driven by in-built technological obsolescence; single driver commuters, company car owners, undertaxed air travellers etc, etc, etc. The benefits of a cleaner environment, car free cities, safer food and water and the diminution of catastrophic global risks, be they environmental, economic or social, seem like small change against the likely and immediate consequences of this project for profit margins, employment and opportunities for unrestricted consumption. Moreover, the potential losers - both producers and consumers - are already politically organised, powerful and entrenched. The immediate beneficiaries of such a programme - pedestrians and cycle manufacturers, the renewable energy industries, organic farmers, future generations - do not amount to much coalition. However, the limits of environmental politics in the West are not solely due to the relative political strengths of the probable short-term winners and losers resulting from the transition to a sustainable economy. Rather, they are deeply ingrained in the culture and beliefs, the everyday modes of thought and ways of life, of Western societies. The character of the environmental threats that we face is collective, long-term and uncertain. While individuals, on the basis of informal risk assessment, are occasionally prepared to abandon destructive individual habits - like smoking - we are unable to make the same call collectively. The immediate health costs and longer term climatic implications of our addiction to petroleum and the motor car are unquestionably of a greater order of magnitude than those of tobacco smoking. But we live in a culture in which the calculus of risk is seen only in individual terms, the time scale of social and political problems barely reaches to the next set of elections, and the community of fate barely extends to our neighbours, let alone distant others and future generations; in these circumstances, prevarication, free-riding, externalisation of costs and short-term self-interest will be the rule.

Even if we were able to alter these ingrained cultural patterns by reason and persuasion, the most sacrosanct folly all remains: our current conceptions of development and growth, and of wealth and wellbeing, are unalterable and unquestionable. As George Bush chillingly stated, before spiking most of the Rio agreements in 1992, 'The American way of life is not up for negotiation'. It is no surprise that one hundred and fifty years of capitalist economic growth has spawned and fed a culture in which more is better, in which the distinction between wants and needs has evaporated, and in which the luxurious is considered essential. What other culture in human history could try and persuade us that the birth of a child requires the purchase of a five-door estate car, a microwave oven, a separate bedroom for balanced psychological development, and the rest of the paraphernalia of Western parenting? At the same time we wilfully disregard our children's environmental inheritance.

But there are some signs of changing attitudes. The international insurance and pension industries are getting worried by climatic change and enormously expensive environmental litigation. Unlike much of the global financial sector they are forced to calculate their profits over the long term and with some regard for the material consequences of investment and growth. In the developing world, despite authoritarian polities and widespread poverty, local and national environmental forces have emerged. International environmental NGOs have become a permanent part of the architecture of global governance. Local resistance to roads, the nuclear industry and landscape destruction is growing in the West as the costs of environmental degradation become inescapable for even the affluent and comfortable. One can detect the subterranean currents of a cultural revolution in the making. The pathologies of Western affluence and overdevelopment are creeping into our consciousness. As every percentage point of growth clicks up, we become more obese or more anorexic, more addicted or more withdrawn. Some of the hottest stocks for the twenty-first century will be in antidepressants and private security. It is becoming apparent that greater personal incomes do not translate into greater happiness; that the index of wellbeing is multifaceted; that the quality of relationships carries more weight than the quantity of consumption. But time is short. This is politics against the clock. The speed at which capitalist development generates environmental threats appears very much greater than the rate at which it nurtures environmental movements. A decade after the publication of the *Communist Manifesto*, and still in relentlessly upbeat mood, Marx wrote, 'mankind always sets itself only such problems as it can solve'. Had Engels a copy of the *State of the World* to hand as he read over the manuscript, he might well have noted in the margin, 'Don't bet on it'.

Emotional Labour

Emotional labour

Pam Smith

The idea to have a special *Soundings* issue on emotions came from conversations about care. The importance of care as a concept, and the changes it has undergone during the restructuring of the welfare state, have been highlighted in previous issues of the journal, notably *The Public Good* (No 4) and *Active Welfare* (No 8). During the Thatcher years, the shift from publicly funded to private care, and the replacement of state provision by the market, resulted in a cultural revolution that has changed the meaning of care. One indicator of this has been the change in language and the reprofiling of emotions in the public domain. On the face of it, 'care' has increasingly entered the arena of our everyday lives. Contract cleaners, identified on the backs of their uniforms as *the care team*, 'wear' it; security firms - *Securicor cares* – 'do' it; and familiars and strangers alike entreat us to *take care*, so implying that we 'do' it for ourselves. When the idea for a special theme on emotions was first mooted, over four years ago, I began to keep a file. Into this file I piled newspaper clippings, articles and photographs which made emotional statements about care. I selected the articles to log a story about emotions. The file has since become an informal logbook, which tracks public displays of emotion in the late twentieth century. I have made a selection from my logbook for this issue of *Soundings*. Together with my commentary, they sketch out some of the changes that have taken place in our cultures of care over the last few years. The source is broadly limited to broadsheets such as the *Guardian, Observer* and *New York Times*.

The link between care and emotions is not new. Hilary Graham powerfully articulated it in the early Thatcher years when she wrote: 'everyday conversations about caring are ... conversations about feelings. When we talk about caring for someone we are talking about our emotion'.[1] Graham is one of a number of feminist writers who have made a key contribution to the understanding of care, exposing its gendered nature and making it visible as labour in both the informal and formal sector. Women are the traditional carers at home and in the work place. With the decline of heavy industry though, the numbers of men engaged in the service sector is also rising. The implication is that, in the post-industrial era of late twentieth century Europe and North America, both men and women are more likely to be involved in relating to people rather than products. The growth in the numbers of unemployed among the traditional male 'breadwinner' also means that men will spend greater periods of time in the home than in the past while more women will enter the workforce.

Arlie Russell Hochschild is an important writer in this field and Stephen Lloyd Smith reviews her work in this issue, starting with *The Managed Heart: the Commercialisation of Human Feeling* (1983). He assesses the contribution Hochschild has made to our understanding of emotions and care in the Euro-American context. Hochschild is an American sociologist who first devised the term 'emotional labour' to describe the way in which two contrasting occupational groups in the USA service sector - flight attendants and debt collectors - managed their emotions to influence the feelings of others. In one case passengers were made to feel safe and cared for in a convivial safe place, while in the other, debtors were made to feel alarmed at the potential consequences of non-payment of bills. Hence flight attendants were portrayed as smiling, friendly, kind and courteous while debt collectors raised their voices and kept their distance.

In later work, Hochschild examined caring and emotions in the home and the interface with paid work. In *The Second Shift* (1989) fifty two-job couples who also cared for children under six were the subjects of study. Hochschild was particularly interested to find out how men and women managed their emotions and whether there were differences. Her enquiries led her to conclude that, despite the rhetoric of gender equality, there had been a *stalled revolution* when it came to child and home care. Equality was cosmetic, with the majority

---

1. H. Graham, 'Caring: a labour of love', in J. Finch and D. Groves (eds), *A Labour of Love: Women, Work and Caring*, 1983.

of women still lacking sufficient help from partners or kin. Despite family friendly policies offered by some employers, investigated in *The Time Bind* (1997), parents were opting to get away from home and the second shift to the more convivial and attractive option of paid work.

In a second essay in this issue, Stephen Lloyd Smith suggests that a theology of emotions can be inferred from Hochschild's work. He shows how emotional labour can be used as an external marker of a caring society, but also to manipulate, manage, exploit and steal the soul. His speculations lead him to ask whether emotions should be considered as 'special' and therefore not for sale, or whether they should be welcomed in the workplace and in the home. If the latter position is adopted then it follows that emotions should be fought for in the same way as one would bargain for mental and manual labour. Furthermore, there is a need to recognise their value and to secure the conditions that sustain emotional labour through adequate remuneration, social and health benefits and the provision of caring spaces and places.

These arguments are not new. Ann Oakley's research in the 1970s revealed housework to be a set of complex skills, which supported the feminist argument that it should be waged.[2] Given women's prominence as carers and house keepers, there has been a certain reluctance on the part of some feminists to emphasise the value of care for fear of making women even more vulnerable to exploitation.

What *is* new about Hochschild's work is that it offers a language for describing invisible work, paid or unpaid, that is taken for granted both in and outside the home. I discovered *The Managed Heart* while studying British student nurses in a health service just beginning to feel the impact of the Thatcher reforms.[3] I then began to use the concept of emotional labour as a device for understanding the processes involved in learning to care, and found that emotionally supportive relationships were vital to the well-being of both students and patients. There were the equivalents of the debt collectors in hospitals too - ward sisters who were hierarchical and critical and instilled fear in students. In short, the conditions for sustaining emotional labour were very clearly visible.

---

2. A. Oakley, *The Sociology of Housework*, Martin Robinson, London 1974.
3. P. Smith, *The Emotional Labour of Nursing: How nurses care*, Macmillan, Basingstoke 1992.

Nursing and health care is one big minefield in the emotional labour stakes. In my log, I make the link between nursing and acting in an exploration of the similarities between these two forms of public performance and emotion management. I have identified occupations other than nursing and acting which require their workers to undertake emotional labour, such as air traffic controllers, doctors, ambulance workers, politicians. Stephen Lloyd Smith mentions others: teachers, the police, social workers, the Samaritans.

It is interesting to speculate as to whether the increased privatisation of the health service will lead to a commercialisation of the emotional labour of nurses and other public sector workers. For example, the images used to recruit nurses, raise money for research and advertise private health packages, always portray the nurse as the key carer, often smiling, always concerned and helpful to patients, their family and friends. Now more than ever, nurses' emotional labour is at a premium, as the numbers of people opting for nursing as a career plummet to an all time low.

The images captured by Dympna Casey in her 'Intensive Care' photo-series go beyond care and concern to reveal anguish and grief, as all efforts to revive a patient fail. We see that as well as being highly technical, intensive care is also intensely emotional. In her picture 'Behind the scenes' we see two nurses sharing a moment of spontaneous emotion, unaware of the camera's gaze. Through their laughter, they hold each other in a caring gesture. Rosy Martin's photo-essay suggests that all carers need these moments so that overwhelming emotions can be contained and held, in order to nurture the 'fragile part of the self' to avoid burn-out.

Sue Williams describes more structured and systematic ways of building support systems into the teaching repertoire of student nurses. She shows how these systems encourage students to make connections between their 'lay' self and their 'professional' self, enabling them to communicate more sensitively. Such support systems are essential if nurses are going to stay in nursing.

I have also included the poem *Miracle on St David's Day*, by Gillian Clarke, because it demonstrates that there are ways other than professional encounters to communicate with patients, even or especially 'the insane'. It shows the power of poetry to make emotional connections in ways that cannot be easily expressed through normal language.

Over the last two decades, major political and social change in Europe and

North America has reduced the state provision of care and increased the burden on personal carers, particularly women. In their essays, Marjorie Mayo, Prue Chamberlayne and Minoo Moallem go beyond the home to situate an analysis of care and emotions within the contemporary socio-political context. Marjorie Mayo makes connections between politics and emotions, unpacking the cosy notions that conceal the sometimes controlling and punitive dimensions of the 'Third Way' associated with New Labour. She describes how, contrary to expectation, Thatcher's children are not hardened individualists accepting the rhetoric of the market unquestioningly. But they do want autonomy and respect. On the advice of his spin doctors, Tony Blair as the voice of New Labour offers a more caring, sharing society. Perhaps this is why when I asked a group of students what they understood by the term 'emotional labour' shortly after Blair had been elected opposition leader, one of them immediately replied *Tony Blair!*

The bigger picture across Europe has seen the collapse of communism, the rolling back of state provision, liberalisation of the marketplace, the fragmentation and casualisation of the workforce, and the development of the contract culture. A variety of third ways have emerged out of these changes, involving the reconfiguring of: public/private; state/voluntary; informal/formal. Prue Chamberlayne and Minoo Moallem give vivid examples of how these reconfigurations impact on the daily lives of carers who navigate and negotiate their own experiences of the Third Way and the realignment of personal and state power.

Prue Chamberlayne presents three case studies from East and West Germany and Britain, which illustrate the changing political cultures of the informal sphere. Each case study provides examples of how different social and political contexts, and the changing role of the state, create different cultures of care which enhance or limit carers' lives and their capacity to care, as well as the lives of those cared for. The different cultures of care are accompanied by the need for different forms of emotion work to manage the care deficit within the domestic arena created by the shortfalls in the public provision of care.

In these accounts the gender dimension is prominent, but, as Prue Chamberlayne observed in discussion, the racial and class dimension of the argument is less apparent. This is because ethnic minority carers are effectively excluded by the system both bureaucratically and personally, which culminates in institutional forms of racism.

Still in Germany, Minoo Moallem, in her essay drawing on the experiences of Iranian immigrant entrepreneurs, puts the racial dimension on the agenda. She shows the blurring of boundaries between public and private, market and home, state and civil society which is caused by the gendered and racialised nature of the relations of care. Minoo Moallem is also keen to challenge Euro-American interpretations of the immigrant experience, which fail to take account of power relations based on gender, class, race and geopolitical location.

This issue of *Soundings* addresses the theme of emotions and their manifestation and management in everyday life. As the articles and images illustrate, emotions are ever present, in politics, the media, at work and in the home. Hochschild provides a language to recognise their varied presentations as emotional labour and the conditions required to sustain it in both the public and private domain.

Arlie Hochschild

Soft-spoken conservationist of emotions

Stephen Lloyd Smith

Stephen Lloyd Smith *reviews the work of Arlie Hochschild, the innovative thinker who first elaborated the concept of emotional labour.*

Intellectual labour is 'nice-work-if-you-can-get it'. Yet the day-to-day work of the academic is mostly taken up with recycling and recombining familiar packages of 'competing ideas'. Very rarely, we are refreshed by persuasive work of stunning originality which not just redefines a problem, but brings us something new and beguiling. We read it and exclaim 'Yes!'. This *buzz* provides a lot of the emotional content to our mostly 'mental' labour.

'Work' was one of those often-revisited and recycled old topics. We used to think about concepts such as 'manual' labour (like digging trenches) and mental labour (like diagnosing faults) we used categories such as 'professional', 'unionised', 'deskilled'... work was sometimes paid, sometimes unpaid (like housework), often 'gendered'.

Into this familiar terrain Arlie Russell Hochschild has introduced a new concern, with the 'sociology of emotions', particularly 'emotional labour', and has established a new vocabulary for thinking about it. She writes exquisitely, in the soft-spoken voice of a conservator of the emotions, a persuasive and yet deceptive ex-Marxist, now turned small-'c' conservative. More to the point, her writing has reached a receptive audience in Middle America a good deal more quickly than the fifteen years it has taken for it to filter through to the 'intellectuals'. (Most textbooks on 'work and organisations' still fail to mention her at all.)

Thanks to Hochschild we're beginning to become concerned with and about emotional labour, paid and unpaid. Concern *is* the word here: concern about the 'commercialisation of human feeling' - the more so if the labourer's smile is not 'just painted on'; concern if feelings of, say, cheery hospitality are *deep-acted* and therefore hard to shrug off at the end of a shift, so that the worker goes home disproportionately and disconcertingly hospitable; concern about the management of 'hearts', hospitable and hostile, among flight attendants and debt collectors; concern with the intrusion of capital into matters private, intimate and heart-felt; concern about the private manipulation of workers by way of addressing their socially derived and widely shared 'feeling rules', to be happy in some settings and sombre in others; concern about a national 'care deficit' in America as the priorities and values of paid work displace those of unpaid domestic care; concern with the emotional disordering of public and private realms; concern that in a bizarre about-turn, work has become an emotional refuge-from-home and 'home has become work' for millions of American women and men; concern that something is going wrong.

The work

Hochschild reached a mass women's magazine audience, in *Cosmopolitan* in 1985, not long after her first major book, *The Managed Heart: the commercialisation of human feeling*, appeared. It bothered her that US airline flight attendants were *commanded* to 'go out there and really smile ... Really *lay it on*.' She wrote:

> This [emotional] labour requires one to induce or suppress feeling in order to sustain the outward countenance that produces the proper state of mind in others ... the sense of being cared for ... This ... calls for co-ordination of mind and feeling, [drawing] on a source of self that we honour as deep and integral to our individuality ... enlightened management realises a separation of display and feeling is hard to keep up over long periods ... Maintaining a difference between feeling and feigning ... leads to strain. We try to reduce that strain by pulling the two closer either by changing the way we feel or by changing what we feign.

When display is required by the job, it is usually feeling that has to change; and when conditions estrange us from our face, they sometimes estrange us from feeling as well.

Here she's concerned as a Marxist conservationist, working to protect workers' authentic inner-selves. But you can also hear a softly-whispered theological protest sounded against those soul-stealing *guests* which the flight attendant is submitted to; against those damn corporate shareholders and against service sector managements: the filthy lucre measuring out sacred hearts into so many pieces of 'customer care'. (More about Hochschild's theological voice in my second article in this issue of *Soundings*.)

Her book *The Second Shift; Working Parents and the Revolution at Home* (1989) was concerned over a 'stalled revolution' for two-job couples with children under 6 years old. Women's working week averaged 15 hours longer than men's. Men were still reluctant to undertake their second shift, and the work place was not a caring place. In conveying this finding, Hochschild was about as welcome as any messenger bringing bad news from the front.

By 1995 she is writing with alarm about a 'care deficit' caused by all kinds of public/private imbalance. Imbalance between the public world of increasingly attractive paid work and the private-and-supposed-to-be-personal world of 'traditional' unpaid care in the home. Imbalance between the withdrawal of the public supply of socialised-and-impersonal care and the high cost of private-and-equally-impersonal 'cold-modern' commercial care. Imbalances which are wished-away altogether in a 'postmodern' pretence that children don't need that much care anyway and may thrive on 'independence'.

Hochschild traced these shifts in the changing content of advice books, such as *Teach Your Child to be Home Alone*, adding '...the image of the "happy" older person also home alone is a disguise of postmodern stoicism.' The same postmodern cosmology 'rids ourselves of the image of mother-and-child and replace[s] it with nothing...' ... 'Warmer notions of "thriving" and "happiness"... go out of fashion, replaced by thinner, more restrictive notions of human well-being ... normalising ... neglect [of] "children in self-care".'

'The cold-modern solution is to institutionalise all forms of human care ... [and] presses for maximum hours and institutional control ... care [which] is the most "practical, efficient, and rational".' She argued that care organisations were maximising care-hours by exploiting the anxieties of 'harried professionals ... "working scared" in the wake of layoffs...', in hotly competitive labour markets. 'The father of a three-month-old child in nine hour day care explained, "I want him to be independent".'

Besides these 'traditional', 'cold-modern', and 'postmodern' models of care, Hochschild describes a fourth, 'warm-modern' model of care: 'It is modern because public institutions have a part in the solution and warm because we do not relinquish all care to them, and because men and women share in what we do not relinquish ... notions of need are not reduced or denied, so caring is recognised as important work ... fulfilling those needs, in part, personally.'

Howwith however a further problem is that paid work is becoming warmer and not just hotter. In *The Time Bind* (1997) Hochschild notes that although parents are aware of accruing 'time' and 'care' deficits to their children, and are aware of their children as 'emotional bill-collectors', warm obligations to work colleagues place parents in a 'time bind'. Despite the best efforts of enlightened managements with 'family-friendly policies', and 'Work-Life Balance Human Resource Management Programmes', Hochschild now finds that neither men nor women show enthusiasm for taking up parenting leave. Home life is seen as less attractive than time spent in places of employment, and more stressful.

Her recent data shows little relationship between the demands of work and the curtailment of care. Workers are not cutting back on home-care, or making use of cold modern care, because of fear about losing their jobs. It is because parents care about paid work too. They experience warmth and care at work. Their revealed and stated preference is to care less about home. 'I'm not supposed to get the office upset,' a mother said. 'Everybody else is putting in forty, fifty, sixty hours.' And another: 'People said to me, "You only took six weeks maternity leave?". I answered, "Gee, guys, that was six weeks I didn't have anybody to talk to. My friends are at work. I am *delighted* to come back."'

As Hochschild observed: 'First *Americo's* workers declared on survey after survey that they were strained to the limit. Second the company offered them policies that would allow them to cut back. Third, almost no one cut back ... Programmes that allowed parents to work undistracted by family concerns were endlessly in demand, while policies offering shorter hours that allowed workers more free or family time languished.'

As the book-jacket explains to the hurrying buyer, '*The Time Bind* exposes the rifts in our crunch time world and reveals how the way we live and work isn't working anymore.'

The conservationist

Hochschild's insight is expansively multi-dimensional, finely separates the effects of each variable and handles detail with care. This is no ordinary conservative reaction to the peculiar blessings of the American Way. Her exciting breakthroughs are:

◆ She gives emotional labour a name. This enables us to notice just how much emotional labour goes on, paid and unpaid.

◆ She demands that emotional labour be paid for at the full value of its associated labour power, even, for example, in 'sacred' work like nursing care. She sounds against treating the emotional content of care as if it was part of the 'natural arts of women' and therefore paying as little for it as for any 'free good', like rain from the sky. Emotional labour needs replenishing rest, sustenance and shelter, she insists. That means wages.

◆ She observes numerous important branches of emotional commodification where service and genuineness is at a premium.

◆ She suggests that emotional labour *absorbs the worker* into the work setting and into the emotional commodities which they are labouring on (with nods and smiles etc) ...

◆ She argues that manual (and presumably mental) labour absorbs comparatively less of the machinist (or say architect), into their respective factory, office and finished pieces.

◆ She understands emotion as the mechanism by which households and corporations connect. In work-rich-but-care-poor-households as in work-rich-and-care-rich-corporations, it's not just the money that's driving things.

◆ She identifies the care deficit as the outcome of the uneven distribution of warmth.

◆ She understands that we gladly surrender to absorption in our quest for 'fulfilment', 'self-actualisation' and 'involvement'.

◆ She sounds warnings from America to the rest-of-the-world.

◆ She enables the asking of new questions. For instance I was prompted to consider what the link is between the business cycle and the demand, availability and supply of different emotions; and to think that consumer *confidence'* and 'economic *depression'* are well named!; perhaps collective emotional shifts cause things to happen 'in the economy'? What a strange thing, to put the term *'caring'* with the word *'profession'* as in 'caring-profession'! And so on ...

◆ She recognises emotion as central to American economy and society.

Neither Etzioni, nor Galbraith - famous worriers about social imbalance - has these startling depths. She makes you stop and think again about the flight attendant's welcome; about the hard-pressed but irresistible, convivial workplace; about the children who miss out on bed-time stories from grandparents; and about sofa-seated, homely daytime TV hosts. It also strikes me that there is a continuity between Hochschild's one-time Marxist concern about the deep-acting flight attendant's emotional absorption in work and her more recent conservative concerns about the care deficit ... that all kinds of workers now show over-absorption in the workplace.

But there is a lot that is unresolved in Hochschild:

◆ Doesn't the appreciative guest re-invigorate the emotional labour rather than steal their soul?

◆ It is hard to see how you can pay for emotional labour without commodifying it and it seems somewhat contrary to then complain that the commodification of emotion is too absorbing. It is hard to see how emotional labour power will be paid for at its value if the setting is not also commercialised.

◆ It is hard to value care as sacred, once commercialised, just as 'love-for-sale' makes no sense.

◆ Why should a nurse in socialised care *care* more than a flight attendant in a commercialised setting? Because public is good and commercial is bad? Is this a safe basis for claiming that the nurse's absorption is good and the flight attendant's is bad? Surely it is more probable that the flight attendant's emotional labour will be paid for at value than the nurse's?

◆ In worrying that emotional labour is *too absorbing*, how can we encourage our children to strive towards fulfilling work as architects or as skilled experts in manufactures, arts and crafts? Why is it a good thing to be absorbed designing a building skilfully, or crafting that building in wood, stone and brick, if absorption is a bad thing? Is the *managed heart* worse than the *managed head* or *managed hand*?

♦ How would the flight attendant reply if told that s/he's more alienated than the factory worker because s/he's absorbed in the task, whereas the factory worker flees from work in a stampede towards the exit gates at the end of each shift?

♦ How come the 'personal' is good, if experienced 'at home', but troubling if experienced 'at work'? What would a policy of making work less absorbing look like? Who would implement it?

My students and I like watching videos of emotional labouring: the *Repomen* who are so well cast for the role; the unusually cheery trainer, teaching sales workers to smile(!) at the *Meadow Hall Shopping Centre*; Mr Gillman, the quintessential undertaker; more sales trainers pushing the *Vwoerk Domestic Home Care System* with bible-thumping passion – 'Welcome to the Family' is their parting comment to the purchaser; *Traffic Wardens* putting up with their dreadful public; and best of all, *Samaritans* doing a night-shift of suicide counselling in Birmingham. Absorbing work makes absorbing video.

There is something particularly magical and captivating about the *Samaritans*. This is gut wrenching, fearful, demanding, heart-destroying, rewarding, exhausting, invigorating, absorbing and skilful, deep-acted emotional labour. The management have arranged the telephone cubicles off a central area for communal rest and recuperation and mutual care. They have thought with great care about sustainability. The counsellors care for each other in bucket-loads, when a voice at the other end of the line threatens the helper by shaking a bottle of pills at them down the phone, or when an anonymous caller slips away into over-dosed oblivion. It brings out the conservative in all of us: our concern with decency, fraternity, sorority, social solidarity and for the people who care.

The point may be that to value care it may have to be treated as sacred; and to value it the most, it may have to be paid the least. Care may become most nonsensical when measured in market values. But why isn't this the case with, say, architecture? The choice between the concern in Hochschild's writing voice, and a straight-forwardly welcoming, secular and matter-of-fact approach to emotional labour, is explored in my second article in this issue.

Bibliography
The Managed Heart: the commercialisation of human feeling, University of California Press, Berkeley 1983.
The Second Shift, Avon, New York 1989.
'The Politics of Culture: Traditional, Cold Modern, and Warm Modern Ideals of Care', in *Social Politics: International Studies in Gender, State and Society* 2,2, 1995.
The Time Bind; When Work Becomes Home and Home Becomes Work, Metropolitan Books/ Henry Holt and Company, New York 1997.

Logging emotions

A logbook of personal reflections

Pam Smith

Pam Smith selects from, and reflects on, the press cuttings on emotions and care which she has been collecting for the last four years.

When the idea for a special *Soundings* theme on emotions was first mooted, over four years ago, I began to keep a file. Into this file I piled newspaper clippings, articles and photographs which made emotional statements about care. The file has since become an informal logbook that tracks late twentieth century public displays of emotion. The logbook is a personal collection of newspaper and magazine clippings which reflect my personal preferences and media biases. The reflections and snippets which follow are based on my collection.

Pilots and politicians

I begin with an article from a *Guardian* front page, written in 1991 under Ministry of Defence reporting restrictions (D. Sharrock, *Guardian*, 19.1.91). In spite of these, it featured testimonies from Gulf War pilots 'in tears' for the loss of fellow crewmembers, and admitting fears of dying. Going on a flying mission was described as 'terribly clinical', requiring the pilot to fly the aircraft 'whatever your emotions'.

Another entry logs the association between emotions and politicians - a piece in the *New York Times* by Maureen Dowd (12.9.93) sub-headed 'When weeping is politically correct'. The report documented a number of key moments when world leaders such as Margaret Thatcher and George Bush shed tears. According to Dowd, 'whether a display of emotion will hurt or help the politician is determined by an exquisitely calibrated set of variables that include sex, circumstance, temperament, amount of water shed, and amount of re-composure time required'. Margaret Thatcher, despite her Iron Lady image 'choked up' when she announced she would not seek re-election, and President Bush was 'teary eyed' at the prospects of sending troops to the Gulf.

More recently the explicit use of emotions has entered the political arena with the advent of the politics of the Third Way. As evidence of this, *The Guardian* carried an article which reported that a new group of psychotherapists were working with politicians with the stated mission of widening 'the political vocabulary so that emotions are open, not hidden' (C. Bennett, *Guardian*, 15.5.96). Not long after the 1997 general election, I watched a television interview between Peter Mandelson and Jeremy Isaacs. The interview might have been living proof that the psychotherapists' mission was being implemented. On reference to his father's death, Mandelson appeared to permit himself a few tears but quickly recovered his composure, giving the audience just enough time to catch a glimpse of him as a caring human being. The recent events surrounding his resignation emphasised another emotional side: that of the cool manipulator of politics and people. Looking through these clippings reveals that a year in politics is indeed a long time!

Emotional labour costs

My log includes a number of observations on nursing, and other occupations which require their workers to undertake emotional labour, such as doctors, ambulance workers and air traffic controllers. I also include material on the link between nursing and acting, as similar forms of public performance and emotion management.

In 1990 the NHS and Community Care Act was introduced which transformed the health and social services beyond all recognition. The Act was based on the premise that a market-led system would encourage competition, improve quality and allow greater consumer choice. Key to the reforms was the introduction of the contract culture based on cost-containment, efficiency and measurable outcomes. At the same time, health care assistants replaced student nurses as the mainstay of the nursing labour force, which allowed them to become college rather than ward based.

Having studied the socialisation of student nurses in the 1980s (i.e. pre-reforms), I was keen to monitor the impact of the changes on nursing and health care.

Some commentators argued, for example, that the introduction of the market to the UK would break the public sector ethos. I was interested in looking at the ways in which emotional labour might become a saleable commodity. As I noted in the introduction to this themed section, images of smiling, concerned and supportive nurses are used to raise money for research, cancer charities, and in advertisements for private health packages.

Scarlet Thomas noted one unexpected consequence of the joint effects of creeping privatisation and the changes in nurse education, in the *Society Guardian* (18.6.97). In her chilling tale of the 'Death of Innocence', she described how the growth of private nursing homes had attracted young women to work there with a minimum of support and training. Those of them who lacked the formal qualifications now required for university-based nurse training chose the nursing homes as an alternative, where they were quickly exposed to death and suffering.

Care on the frontline

A study of morale amongst community nurses and health visitors in the early years of the reforms found that frontline staff were beginning to experience conflicts between the financial concerns of their managers and caring for patients and clients (M. Traynor and B. Wade, *The morale of nurses working in the community: A study of three NHS trusts: Year 3*, Daphne Heald Research Unit, RCN, London 1994).

A health visitor expressed her consternation at the change: 'Money has replaced the patient in our focus of care. We need to resist this insidious erosion to our commitment to people' (p43).

Managers, on the other hand, believed that a 'business ethos' was highly compatible with the principles of good health care and criticised nurses for being too emotional and involved to make rational decisions and set priorities. By distancing themselves from the frontline, managers were unlikely to see the consequences on staff of their cost-cutting measures.

Valerie Stinson, writing in *The Guardian Weekend* (July 1994) showed how the simple but highly symbolic measure of closing hospital canteens during the night and replacing the catering staff by vending machines took away 'the feeling of support junior doctors used to get on late shifts'. Stinson placed this withdrawal of a space for mutual support in the context of the extreme stress junior hospital doctors were said to be under, and the lack of opportunities for them to talk to their seniors about their plight, for fear of jeopardising their future career prospects.

A student nurse in my study (*The Emotional Labour of Nursing*, Macmillan 1992) expressed a similar reluctance to admit the need for support: 'There just happened to be a little girl on the ward who had cancer and for some reason she took to me, her mother did and her family did too. She was six and she died in the end. It all got a bit much really. None of the trained staff actually asked me if I was managing. They think that 'cos you're a nurse you can manage. Outwardly you might be managing but I used to go home and cry my eyes out.'

How did she learn to manage? The NHS charm school described below could be seen as one approach.

The NHS charm school

The use of 'Hello' nurses is another example of how emotional labour is being reformulated to meet the market needs of the new NHS - as is the institution of the roving ambulance services documented in the subsequent section.

In March 1996 the *London Evening Standard* ran an article entitled 'Welcome to the NHS charm school' (C. Bassingdale, 12.3.96). The charm school offered training sessions in 'customer care' to all members of the health care team in order to 'reduce aggravation, cope with abuse and deal with difficult situations'.

When asked to comment on the introduction of the charm school, a British Medical Association (BMA) spokesperson was doubtful that the 'private sector ethos can be grafted onto the NHS ... because it just doesn't work. The NHS is built on the ethos of caring; the private sector on profit. Attempts to mix the two lead to clashes'.

The Hello Nurses

In June and July of the same year the *Sunday Times* and *The Guardian* reported on the publication of the hospital league tables (L. Rogers and S. Hamilton,

Sunday Times, 30.6.96; D. Brindle, *Guardian*, 3.7.96). One of the performance ratings was related to waiting times in the Accident and Emergency department. A number of hospitals achieved high ratings because they had allegedly employed a new type of nurse to greet and assess patients within five minutes of their arrival. The press dubbed them the Hello nurses. A chief executive complained that 'because of the large number of patients seen, this process consists simply of a visual assessment. It fails to provide any meaningful benefit to patients'.

A few days later a patient who was also a journalist gave evidence that confirmed the chief executive's view. He reported his own sorry experience in the Accident and Emergency department of a top-rated hospital. Following a stabbing injury he was greeted within five minutes but then had to wait a gruelling ten hours without explanation in a weak and debilitated condition. He concludes: 'The mindless violence of the original (screwdriver) attack had depressed me greatly; my five-star NHS treatment made it worse' (E. Pilkington, Guardian,19.9.96).

Decentralising the ambulance services

My next example relates to another newspaper report, this time on the effects of decentralising the ambulance services in one trust. I have chosen this example because it demonstrates the negative effects of streamlining an organisation for staff - although initial reports are that the reorganisation is better for patients. A *Guardian* article entitled 'Emergency Measures' quoted the manager of an NHS ambulance trust as thinking 'it is bad management, not lack of money that results in a poor service (H. Martin, *Guardian*, 7.8.97). Acting on this assumption, the ambulance crews were dispersed away from the centre to wait for calls in key areas, losing the 'comfort and camaraderie of the ambulance stations', away from toilet facilities and hot drinks. The opinion of the local union representative was that there had been a great improvement for patients but that the work conditions of staff had deteriorated. One staff member expressed his dissatisfaction with the changes by indicating that he'd opt for stacking shelves in Sainsburys for the same pay.

Although these examples are anecdotal, they serve as powerful indicators of how emotional labour can be used to commercialise rather than support care. There is also a recognition by staff representatives that patients and profits don't mix.

It is only a question of time before the 'Hello' nurses and the ambulance crews described above vote with their feet. Indeed my most recent log, from a *Guardian* headline of 29 December 1998, read 'Nursing crisis looms'. Nurses were reported to be leaving the profession in their thousands because of poor pay and conditions.

Air Traffic Controllers

I want to say a word about the air traffic controllers who have been in the news recently with all those near misses. My first log appears in July 1996 when a *Guardian* article (H. Gould, *Guardian* 13.7.96) caught my attention about the work of air traffic controllers. The article was a brisk and efficient account of what was required for a career in air traffic control, emphasising the people element of the job. It was for 'people who want to fly people - requiring nerves of steel, confidence and quick thinking'. There were reassurances that although the job was stressful counselling and camaraderie were at hand. By August 1998, the story was quite different. An *Observer* article headlined 'Panic over mid-air misses' gave a chilling account of a near-miss mid-air collision in which there had been less than a minute to prevent the death of hundreds of passengers (J. Walters, *Observer*, 23.8.98). A senior controller was coaching a trainee when the incident happened. Reasons for the increasing number of near mishaps included increasingly crowded skies and cramped working conditions. The emotional labour element here is that the system was so under pressure that at least one of the controllers stayed on duty rather than going home, which was the recognised procedure. The controllers were neither talked to nor counselled about the incident, and were left feeling guilty and unable to sleep for two nights. Speed-up in the workplace is a problem for most workers, not only for air traffic controllers - and it squeezes out the emotional support required to do a sound and safe job.

Holding the line
Learning to do emotional labour

Stephen Lloyd Smith asks elsewhere in this journal whether emotions are special, and whether emotional labour occupies a similar status to mental and manual labour. Is there a need to recognise the value of emotions, and to secure the conditions that sustain them, such as adequate remuneration, social and health benefits and the provision of caring spaces and places? The log so far suggests that there is such a need, because it indicates that emotions *are* special.

Returning to the student nurse from *The Emotional Labour of Nursing* - how did she learn to cope and to manage her feelings? On being asked this she replied: 'I've found that at work you can't be cross even though you feel like it, you've got to be reasonably under control. You've got to learn to switch off and be different when you go home.'

When again asked how she did it, she said 'by trial and error'. This raised the question of whether this way of learning put her at risk of becoming detached and alienated. Are there ways in which the student could learn - through experience and systematic training - to use her feelings to remain therapeutically involved?

Hochschild's account of emotional labour suggests that there are. There are two kinds of emotional labour, achieved by either deep or surface acting. The flight attendants in Hochschild's study received intensive training to manage their emotions in a variety of situations. With surface acting workers were more likely to feel inner dissonance, because they were 'putting on a face' or feigning their emotions. More experienced workers were found to be particularly adept at deep acting which enabled them to distinguish between 'personal' and 'work' selves and protected them from burn-out.

A senior staff nurse in my study was able to do the same. She described nurses as actresses who left their personal self at the door before going on 'stage' in the ward. In this way she was able to protect the patients from her feelings, but also herself by not revealing her mood to them: 'I very very rarely bring any kind of a mood to the ward because I believe we are actresses as well. The minute we hit that door that's the stage, we're on show and that's the way I've always been. I have gone into work depressed but the minute I go in the door the smile's on my face and the patients don't know because I'm an actress as well.'

The performing arts or the art of the possible

I was interested to find that actors often described their work in a similar way to the staff nurse.

Performance requires research, and Robbie Coltrane, as forensic psychologist

Fitz for the 1994 TV series *Cracker*, was so convincing in the role that he was phoned up for advice. Coltrane comments: 'It's an illusion, and the trick is to make it look as real as possible. If people think I have greater insight into human psychology now, just as, at the end of *Tutti Frutti* they thought I was a good rock and roll singer in love with Suzi Kettle, then I've done my job' (*Guardian Guide*, 1994)

'The minute I go in the door the smile's on my face because I'm an actress as well'

Susie Blake is more explicit on the link between performance and emotions. Referring to her drama teacher-director Norman Ayrton she says: 'He taught us to intellectualise what we were feeling, so we could reproduce our emotions on the stage. This is the most important lesson I've learnt. When you first act you use your own emotions, you really feel it and don't intellectualise at all. But this gives an unclear message to your audience and is also impossible to keep up night after night - you will literally crack up.

Norman taught me that it is our job to take people out of themselves - not to have an emotional, tearjerk session. When you go to the theatre you hope to feel something, whether it be anger, sadness or joy. If you go to watch a load of actors having an orgy on the stage you will think, "Well they enjoyed it but I didn't"' (E. Moore, 'Talkback', Susie Blake, Guardian, 14.5.96).

Labour conditions

What then are the conditions which permit the production and reproduction of emotional labour, to make it visible and valued in the workplace, over and above individual performance? Prior to the NHS reforms, one way of ensuring favourable labour conditions lay with the ward sister or charge nurse (her male equivalent), who as the architect of nursing work and organisation set the emotional tone. Student nurses moved through the wards on a regular basis, providing a cohesive workforce. When students and staff nurses felt appreciated and emotionally supported by the ward sister, they not only had a role model for emotionally explicit patient care; they also felt able to care for patients in this way.

As one student put it: 'When I know that the ward sister cares then I feel a bit more at ease.'

Sisters were seen as critical to morale because of their influence not only on how students and staff nurses worked but also how they *felt*.

A patient told me: 'If staff work well with sister then the atmosphere of the ward is well. They shouldn't be frightened of her.'

As R.W. Revans showed over thirty years ago (in *Standards for Morale: Cause and Effect in Hospital*, Nuffield Trust, OUP 1964), hospitals with high morale had effective communication systems, ward sisters who spoke often with junior nurses, a stable workforce and rapid patient recovery. Now the picture has changed. Ward sisters and charge nurses spend more time on budgets and bureaucracy and less time on direct parent and staff contact. The combined effects of educational change and the recruitment crisis means that students are less visible on the wards to provide a coherent workforce. Problems of retention have led to hospitals being staffed by large numbers of agency nurses who often don't know the patients and staff. As Steve Hams, a staff nurse, concludes, 'It is obviously much better to have continuity of care so nurses build up relationships with patients, and with colleagues' (quoted in *The Guardian*, 29.12.98). But as long as low pay and poor conditions persist, morale is unlikely to improve and problems of staff recruitment will continue.

Impossible conditions

My final log concerns the emotion management required to balance the multiple job-holding which is a phenomenon of an increasingly casualised workforce, of which agency nurses are a part. Articles from the *New York Times* (P.B. Noble, 19.9.93) and *The Guardian* (J. Green and J. Upton, 14.1.98) present a picture of a workforce under threat. Women and people of colour are particularly pressurised as they balance a variety of jobs that, because they are temporary and casualised, are unlikely to carry benefits such as sick pay, holiday entitlements and pension rights. In a US survey, burnout was widespread and workers felt guilty about taking time for themselves at the expense of their work and family. The report concluded that: 'Carving out some time for oneself represents an investment in mental health and well being that may well offset occasional or modest reductions in attention to work and family.'

This logbook tells a tale of mixed emotions in a variety of public arenas. Most striking is the deterioration of working conditions and wages in the public sector. References to research even ten years ago shows that, although the public sector was always starved of resources, there were then still caring spaces and places for the production and reproduction of emotional labour. This log testifies to the loss of those spaces and places. In this age of increasing privatisation and individualisation, the performing arts, or the art of the possible, offer opportunities for recognising emotions as special; but we also must recognise that emotional labour entails labour costs which need to be fiercely defended and fought for, at home and in the workplace (for, as the song says, 'You don't know what you've got 'til it's gone').

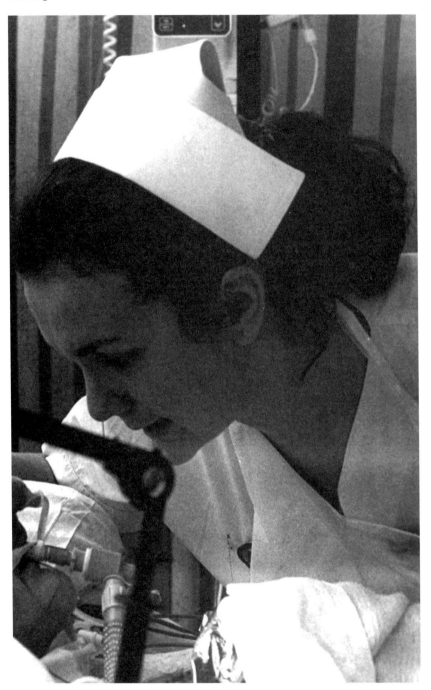

Intensive Care

Photoessay by Dympna Casey

Photography implies the recognition of a rhythm in the world of real things. What the eye does is find and focus on the particular subject within the mass of reality, what the camera does is simply to register on film the decision already taken by the eye.

Cartier Bresson

Photography is about communicating ideas and experiences as well as information. The photographs presented here explore and describe nursing. With the aid of the camera the personalities, environments, emotions and above all the varied relationships in nursing are revealed. It is hoped that the viewer will be drawn to view these photographs again and again finding new associations and new interpretations.

Dympna Casey

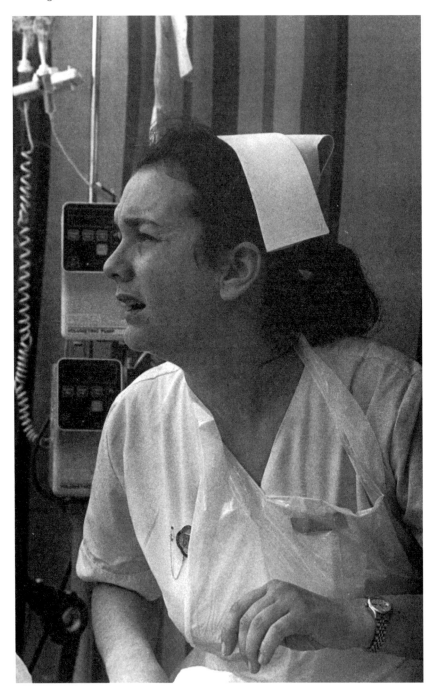

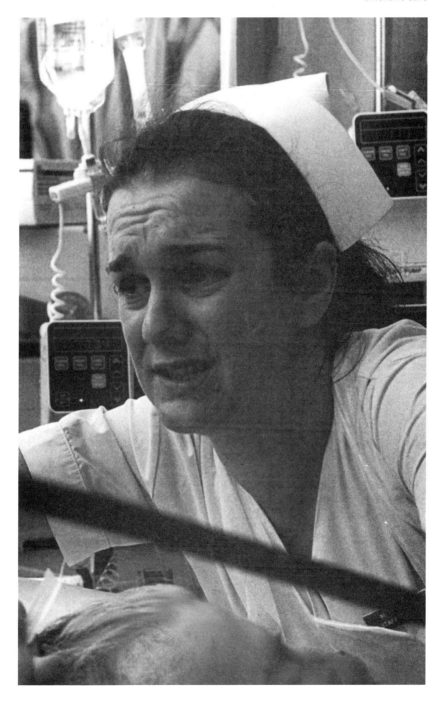

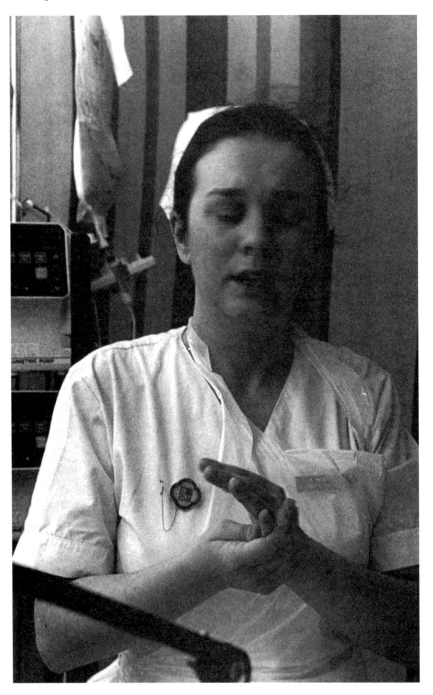

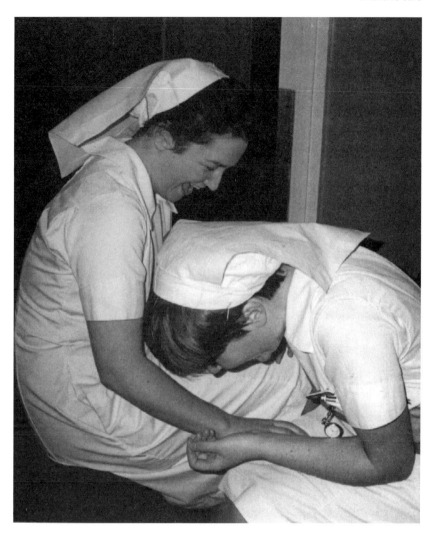

A lighter moment from a different series: 'Behind the scenes'

New language: New Labour

Exploring the politics of emotions

Marjorie Mayo

Marjorie Mayo *looks at New Labour's use of the language of the emotions.*

From the vantage point of its closing years, the politics of emotions emerge as one of the key themes of twentieth century history. Commenting on the century, Raymond Firth has argued that although the technological developments were significant, the most significant development, in terms of ideas, was 'the change from a relatively rational and scientific view of things to a non-rational and less scientific one'.[1] As Hobsbawm's history, the *Age of Extremes*, has argued, this has been a century of unparalleled technological and material progress - and the most murderous barbarism, with genocide justified by fascist ideologies rooted in a hatred for the eighteenth century Enlightenment, and a belief in 'the superiority of instinct and will' over 'reason and rationalism'.[2]

The point is not, of course, to suggest that bringing emotions into politics necessarily leads to the triumph of barbarous instincts (although there are disturbing enough examples, both more recently and closer to home - Enoch

---

1. R. Firth, cited in E. Hobsbawm, *Age of Extremes*, Michael Joseph, London 1994, p2.
2. *Age of Extremes*, p117.

Powell's overtly racist 'Rivers of Blood' speech, just to mention one particularly infamous case) but to sound a warning note about the potential dangers. The point to emphasise is simply this - that bringing emotions into politics is neither new nor politically neutral. It is a phenomenon which needs to be explored further - unpacking the political implications, in any given context.

How, then, to unravel the particularities of the politics of emotion in Blair's Britain, and the politics of the 'Third Way'? This article argues that emotions in general, and 'caring' more specifically, have particular roles to play in the problematic politics of the 'Third Way'. Emotions have their part in the presentation of political agendas - as in the spin-doctoring of New Labour's alternative to the agendas of the New Right: New Labour offers an ideology of individual choice, but in a more caring society - squaring the circle; it offers liberalism with equality of opportunity, capitalist economics with socialist politics. 'Life' politics adds the politics of personal emotions and relationships to the ideology of the 'Third Way'. Agendas of caring are part and parcel of this whole legitimisation process. This applies to the politics of New Labour in general, and also to the politics of welfare re-organisation, and community care more specifically.

But the politics of emotions are fraught with tensions and contradictions. For example, the reverse side of the caring coin may be controlling, especially in the context of welfare state reforms. And the processes of legitimation bring their own added complications. 'Life' politics, which may seem a bland concept, has the potential for raising aspirations - including aspirations for individual choice and respect - aspirations which cannot readily be met within current welfare spending constraints.

The politics of emotion have already been criticised from the Right. The authors of *Faking It*, for example, have argued, in place of sentimentality, for a return to more traditional values, with more emphasis upon self-discipline and a stiff upper lip - less individual choice and more individual responsibility.[3] Their critique will be outlined in this article, since much of it is pertinent (although very different conclusions are drawn). The article then concludes by raising some of the questions to be addressed to explore the possible bases of alternative critiques from the left.

---

3. D. Anderson and P. Mullen, *Faking It*, The Social Affairs Unit, London 1998.

The politics of emotion, 'life politics' and the 'Third Way'

Critics have pointed to the vagueness and vapidity of the 'Third Way' - it is 'flexible' and 'innovative' 'like Clinton's definition of sexual relations', in the view of Francis Wheen (*Guardian*, 23.9.98) - meaning all things to all men, if not to all women. The 'Third Way' has been presented as the 'New Politics for the New Century' - uniting democratic socialism and liberalism, rights and responsibilities, individual liberty in the market economy with mutual obligations, and a concern for equality of opportunity and social justice. But too often it glosses over differences, a task which is made easier through the imprecision of its language. And critics argue that this blurring of concepts is an inherent weakness of third way politics.

Chantal Mouffe's article in the summer 1998 issue of *Soundings* exposes the key contradictions of the 'Third Way'. As she so clearly argues, its attempt to blur the left/right divide actually 'creates a democratic deficit and leads to the trivialisation of political discourse' (p15). This leads, for example, to a preoccupation with the unmasking of sex scandals, in place of genuine debate around alternative political agendas. As Mouffe concludes, the mistaken belief that political antagonisms have disappeared is linked to New Labour's inability to accept the expression of dissent within its own ranks. 'Its authoritarianism chimes with its conception of a consensual politics of dialogue from which strife has been eliminated' (p23).

Rather than repeating existing critiques of the 'Third Way', the focus here is upon the connections with 'life politics', emotions and caring. The 'Third Way' seems to promise that we can have our cake and eat it, once conflicts between left and right have been removed from the political scene. The promise is the attainment of a new and more caring society, passionate in its commitment to social justice and social community - and all to be pursued within the framework of the tax and spend constraints of the previous government. The caring values are central here - the soothing smile legitimising the restructuring of the welfare state, within the framework of New Right economic policies.

So what is new? After all, the previous government attempted to legitimise the increasing marketisation of welfare in apparently fairly similar ways. Emotive terms such as 'Care' and 'Community' were used to touch chords. The NHS and Community Care package seemed to offer more in terms of caring, as well as in terms of respect and choice. But although there are similarities, there do seem to be differences. The previous government was clear about the politics involved - the free-market politics of the New Right.

In contrast some 'Third-Wayers' such as Giddens - who is often described as the Blairites' guru - have located their project somewhat differently, as being beyond left and right (although Blair himself, in his pamphlet, *The Third Way* (Fabian society 1998), locates the New Politics as being on the centre left). Giddens, in his book *Beyond Left and Right: The Future of Radical Politics* (Polity 1994), starts from the position that both socialism and conservatism have become moribund, whilst neo-liberalism has become increasingly paradoxical - weighed down with its own internal contradictions. Giddens characterises the new emancipatory politics as 'life politics'. This is a politics of identity and choice, a politics which includes areas which were previously considered outside the political sphere altogether. 'Life politics' is not, of course, to be equated with the politics of emotion. Nor is it, according to Giddens - or not only - a politics of the personal. But these personal and emotional aspects are included - feminist and ecological concerns for example - as well as the more orthodox areas of political involvement such as work and economic activity. The new politics, in Giddens's view, includes more reflexivity, and greater involvement and choice, with less respect for tradition and more dialogue, including increasingly dialogic relations in personal life, between marriage partners for example, and between parent and child - a democracy of the emotions. The politics of emotion thus seems to be, in this version of the third way, closely implicated in the move away from the politics of left and right.

Giddens himself accepts that the changes he describes can have negative as well as positive outcomes. But these varying implications are not explored in terms of left/right political alternatives. On the contrary, 'life politics' is defined as being beyond both left and right. This potentially leads to precisely the type of 'politics without adversary' which Mouffe rejects so emphatically. The critics argue that this 'Third Way', as set out in Blair's pamphlet, or indeed in Giddens latest book of the same name, blandly evades the crucial issues of the day. 'This is not Das Kapital or the Constitution of Liberty; it's more an odyssey by Candide', it has been suggested, with everything for the best, in the best of all possible worlds (D. Walker, *Guardian*, 22.9.98). The point of being critical of this approach, as Mouffe has also emphasised, is not to argue for a return to traditional solutions. Increasing emotional democracy does has a positive ring (whatever it may actually mean in practice) as do increasing respect, greater reflexivity and choice. Rather, the point is to disentangle the differing political implications, before making choices - taking sides in fact.

Critiques from the right

There have, of course, been critiques of the new emotionalism in the public arena from the right - the 'sentimentalisation of modern society' as the editors of *Faking It* describe it. Anderson and Mullen object to the debasing of terms such as 'community', 'long after neighbourliness has left the community' (pp4-5). They define the sentimentalist as a person in denial; 'and what he avoids or denies is reality … He likes to think that good ends can be achieved without unpleasantness' (p 5). In a chapter in the book on sentimentality in modern literature, Robinson adds D. H. Lawrence's definition - sentimentality as 'working off on yourself feelings you haven't really got' (p121). This cannot, of course, be directly equated with Giddens's 'life politics' or the politics of emotion in relation to the 'Third Way' more generally. But *Faking It* does make some connections. Steyn's chapter on sentimentality in the media, for example, specifically criticises Clinton, Gore and Blair for propagating the new sentimentalised, media-digestible politics, characterised by spin, image and gesture rather than substance. This is not, Steyn argues, an instance of the feminist slogan the personal is political; it is more a 'drag-queen travesty of what the women's movement intended' (p179) - style rather than political philosophy. Steyn predicts that Gore's electoral campaign will entail 'more human interest stories, more teary celebrities, more false empathy, and more debasement of public debate, presided over by masters of humbug in politics and media alike' (p179).

O'Hear' s much quoted chapter on Diana similarly defines her sentimentality in terms of her refusal to face up to reality. Diana wanted to have her cake and eat it, according to O'Hear, wanting to be both extraordinary and ordinary, as the jet-setting mother of the future king, who rejected protocol, pursuing her chosen role as the queen of hearts. There are potential parallels here too - the Third Wayers' refusal to face the reality of political choices. O'Hear's conclusions, however, like those of his fellow authors, are firmly traditionalist. Tony Blair stands accused of colluding in 'the elevation of feeling above reason, caring above principle, personal gratification above commitment and propriety' ... and the '"People" over rank, tradition and history' (p190). *Faking It* argues for a return to the traditional values of the right, based upon real religion, stoicism where necessary and personal responsibility.

Exploring left alternatives

As it has already been suggested, the politics of emotion are fraught with tensions and contradictions. Like the Thatcherite policies on caring which preceded them, the politics of the 'Third Way' are also potentially controlling. The authoritarian strands within New Labour's thinking can be identified, too, in the politics of emotions.

On the other hand, the processes of legitimation have also been fraught with tensions and contradictions. Legitimation is generally unlikely to be secured through the use of propaganda alone - without substance which relates to people's actual interests and aspirations. So, for example, 'Care in the Community' policies could be presented as justifiable in part, at least, because the claims which were made for community care resonated with popular mistrust of large-scale institutional care. Whatever the shortcomings of the reality of care, in the mixed economy of welfare, there were popular aspirations for alternatives, which were more caring - with more respect and choice for individuals and their families and carers.

It has been argued that the ideological offensive of the Thatcher years was actually resulting in a sea change in popular attitudes - changing the nation's psyche. The new generation of 'Thatcher's children' were said to be growing up to be more selfish, individualistic, assertive and market-oriented - and correspondingly less caring, or collectivist, in outlook. In practice, the weight of evidence seems more ambiguous, pointing in potentially different directions.

As the Trades Union Congress 1996 study of young people's attitudes demonstrated, young people are certainly less prepared to accept authority unquestioningly. They are more sceptical. And they want to be treated fairly and with respect. They do value autonomy and choice. But this does not at all mean that they have rejected collectivism - on the contrary, the majority of those interviewed in the TUC study, *Young People and Employment*, believed, for example, that trade unions are essential to protect workers' interests. These findings are in line with the findings from British Social Attitudes Surveys. Young people do understandably have aspirations - like the rest of the population, they would like to be treated with respect, and to have more individual choice. But this does not at all mean that they have necessarily bought the rhetoric of the market, lock stock and barrel. On the contrary, there is a continuing battle of political ideas to be fought. And this includes struggling around the competing ideas which are inherent in the politics of emotion.

One hundred and fifty years on, the Communist Manifesto contains passages which still have potential relevance here. The development of capitalism has torn asunder the old ties, the Communist Manifesto argued, leaving only self-interest and the cash nexus.

> The bourgeoisie, wherever it has got the upper hand, has put an end to all feudal, patriarchal, idyllic relations. It has pitilessly torn asunder the motley feudal ties that bound man to his 'natural superiors', and has left remaining no other nexus between man and man than naked self-interest, than callous 'cash payment'. It has drowned the most heavenly ecstasies of religious fervour, of chivalrous enthusiasm, of philistine sentimentalism, in the icy water of egotistical calculation. It has resolved personal worth into exchange value, and in place of the numberless indefeasible chartered freedoms, has set up that single unconscionable freedom - Free Trade (Lawrence and Wishart, Marx and Engels Selected Works, 1968, p38).

If the development of the cash nexus was already so remarkable a hundred and fifty years ago, should the more recently-identified tendency towards the marketisation of emotions really cause us further surprise? Or indeed, the use of emotions and sentiment to veil the underlying realities of social relations which are exploitative and oppressive?

Marx and Engels were not, of course, arguing for a return to traditional ties and values. On the contrary. The Communist Manifesto is deeply critical of programmes which attempt to turn the clock back, or (sentimentally?) fail to start from a realistic analysis of contemporary realities, whether these attempts come from the right or from the Utopian left. There are also, perhaps, potential parallels between Marx and Engels' criticisms of those Utopians and more recent comments on the Third Wayers - those who endeavour 'to deaden the class struggle and to reconcile class antagonisms'

(Communist Manifesto p61), who dream of realising schemes for building 'castles in the air', rather than starting from a critical analysis of these conflicting interests, as the basis for developing realistically grounded strategies for social transformation.

The logic of Marx and Engels' analysis would not, in any case, suggest that there could be any realistic possibility of a return to 'real' emotions, 'authentic' emotions, as these have been traditionally portrayed. If human consciousness develops as people interact with their material and social environment, as Marx and Engels argued, then human feelings and emotions can also develop, whether positively or negatively (depending upon the viewpoints of those concerned). Such a view of humans as social beings - social actors inhabiting a world which is socially constructed - is, of course, consistent too, with a range of other social scientists' perspectives.

If human nature is not forever fixed, then a range of possible future alternatives is open. Human emotions can, of course, be manipulated for barbarous ends. But so, conversely, could there be a socialist politics which includes the aim of replacing the marketisation of emotions with the construction of emotional democracy.

Theology of Emotion

Stephen Lloyd Smith

Stephen Lloyd Smith *explores further the concept of emotional labour.*

Day in the life

On 5 December we encountered a salesman who had something about him. It was *partly* that he looked out of place in his business suit, scraping ice off the car we fancied test-driving. Perhaps none of the sales staff were expecting custom anyway, not at 8:30am in freezing weather. After running through the car's service history, he volunteered that he was a qualified nurse, now 'switching to medical sales'. 'Nursing is all about care and trust', he continued, 'and medical sales should be about people having confidence in your promises. 'Both jobs are out here,' he explained without any prompting, pointing to a space in the air. 'So they've put me "on placement" in car sales for a while, which is about *just the opposite'*, now gesturing in the other direction. He could 'see the sense of it' and so could I. He could not have been clearer: hospitality rather than hostility in each job; the sacred in nursing, the sacred and the profane in sales; one job public, the other two commercial, but conducted in semi-public. His unprompted confession was touching. I think his story was for real as he was far more 'nurse' than 'salesperson'. He talked about 'familiar feelings we all have for the old car'.

In the afternoon we experienced help and a warm welcome from the family of a particularly helpful work colleague. I needed to get a motorcycle fixed and qualified for assistance as 'one biker to another'. As this biker dealt with my back wheel with confidence, it all felt several degrees better than Very Good. He stops his priceless collection of tools from being stolen, he said, by 'caring for his neighbours, particularly the "iffy" one'.

In the evening we were back in the realm of commercial and public emotional labour as part of a well-heeled audience for a rock and roll stage revue, which didn't quite 'work'. You could see all the effort that was put into the stage design, the choreographic and musical performance. The audience applauded in all the right places, but too readily. Rock and roll is now sacred and hospitable; this show conveyed neither. The effect wasn't helped by the pungent, death-like perfumes circulating from some women seated in front of us. The performance was both intricate and demanding. They'd done everything faultlessly, but left us cold. It was too well cued, right down to the scripted embroidery which the performers gave to our final ovation.

Our days are full of episodes like these. They mostly pass unnoticed.

After rambling discussion about 'alienation', 'morale' and 'motivation', commentators on work are waking up to the puzzling question of 'the passions'. Hochschild's brilliant essays on the emotional divisions of labour among flight attendants and debt-collectors, and between households, places of employment and care, have given other writers fresh insights into ways of looking at: organisations and the individuals within them; 'stress' and nursing care; gender; dying and bereavement.[1]

The Managed Heart launched my collection of items on 'emotional labour': the work done on and through feelings, by bailiffs, soldiers, undertakers, sales workers, tour guides, prostitutes, politicians and the like - work that's sacred or profane, hospitable or hostile, public or private, emotions which are deeply felt or superficially acted.

Taken together, the collection *adds up* to something, hinting at an enigmatic, pervasive though veiled, Western, *theology of emotion*. I think this theology has anaesthetised many of us, veiling emotional labour; at the same time some of

---

1. See for example: J. Duncombe and D. Marsden, 'Love and Intimacy: The Gender Division of Emotion and Emotion Work; A Neglected Aspect of Sociological Discussion of Heterosexual Relationships', in *Sociology*, 27, 1993; S. Fineman, *Emotions in Organisations*, Sage, London 1993; S. Jackson, 'Even Sociologists Fall in Love: An Exploration in the Sociology of Emotions' in *Sociology* 27, 1993; N James, 'Emotional labour, skills and work in the social regulation of feeling', *Sociological Review*, 37,1989; T. Newton, S. Fineman and J. Handy, *Managing Stress: Emotion and Power at Work*, Sage, London 1995; P. Smith, *The Emotional Labour of Nursing*, Macmillan, Basingstoke 1992; T. Walter, (1990) *What Makes a Good Funeral?*, Hodder, London 1990.

the contradictions in what Hochschild says (see my other essay in this section of *Soundings*) seem to stem from this theology.

The self-defining self

> The mind is its own place, and in itself
> Can make Heav'n of Hell, a Hell from Heav'n
>
> Milton, *Paradise Lost*, Book I

A twentieth century picture of the self leaps from these eighteen words. Milton sees us defining the place we find ourselves in, determining it as heavenly or hellish. This unfolds into a view of subjective life, currently in vogue, animated by 'actors' busy 'creating meaning' through 'consciousness'. Next out is the 'cognitive approach' to depression, which centres exactly on the 'subjective meanings' which depressives make of their hellish places. Milton anticipates current subjectivist writing in suggesting that there's little point to exploring 'objective' Hells and empirical Heav'ns, as if these existed 'out there' to be measured. What matters to him is the way it all looks to each of us.

But there is something in this quote which many twentieth century readers may determinedly ignore: *emotion*. Heaven and Hell are not just any old kind of cerebral 'meaning' - a 'subjective-perspective', or 'viewpoint', 'understanding', 'construct' or 'orientation' … They are full-on, urgent, fulsome, ghastly, glorious and gutsy *emotional* states. In comparison with modern jargon about self - which abounds with optical and cerebral metaphor like 'perspective' - Milton's take on subjectivity as Heav'nly and Hellish makes present conceptions look feeble.

Emotional stuff is being extracted from workforces as the stuff of significant sections of the economy. Hochschild reckons that a third of the US workforce are direct workers on the emotions. As customers, we pay for the stuff and know when we get it. We also know when we give it without payment or without the expectation of payment, and Westerners experience it daily in the shifting tone of organisations and households, and in their variable subjective *buzzing*. Emotion is fully functioning private and social capital.

So why not measure emotional range, intensity, modulation, variation, accentuation, expression, attenuation, interaction and control, across all kinds of settings: in public and private domains; in sacred and profane encounters, either deeply-felt or superficially acted; between hospitable and hostile work; in passionate, passionless, emotionally constraining and containing, bruising or happy organisations? Why is it not being classified, measured, calibrated, dissected, recorded, categorised, compared and contrasted; why are we not pinpointing the necessary conditions for producing the stuff; understanding the limits of supply; asking whether and how output as a whole has risen or fallen; linking economic and emotional *depression?* How is its production and consumption 'broken down by age and sex', by ethnicity and class; what do we require by way of rest and shelter in order to be able to produce more of the stuff tomorrow. Below follow some examples which illustrate the kind of 'stuff' emotional labour is made of.

Cunning shop-floor resistance

'John' was visiting the United States and went shopping out of necessity. Joining a long checkout queue he had time to study the till-operator's cheery *have-a-nice-day* routine. As his turn came closer, her misplaced familiarity bothered him.

By the time he's about to be served John's ready: 'Look, I'm not a company spy or anything', he begins, 'and I'm not going to tell on you and get you into trouble for not doing it. I know it's a *management thing* that means you've got to do it; but please, there's no need for that *greeting.*' The operator listens without making eye contact, staring blankly ahead, chewing gum. John continues, 'It's not that I *dislike* you or anything, we just don't know each other … never met … and probably won't meet again. … strangers eh? So I'd prefer it if … well, if you … don't wish me a *Nice Day* and so on…'

The operator is waiting on her turn in the conversation. When it comes, she pauses, turns and looks him straight in the eye: 'Have a nice day - *you SHMUK!*"

Milton might have collected this for *his* files; it's hard to make checkout work Heav'nly, he might admit and it might be Hellish. But this creative *Mind* is managing her customers, *Making* the *Place* she finds herself *In* and demarcating her *Own Place* within it. Her knowing superficiality is spelled out to both her customers and herself. She refuses to give her self to her work and until she encounters this alien, assumes that everybody understood urban guile as 'fair enough'. Her shop floor resistance heads off demands from employer and customers alike, to put her feelings into the work, surrendering herself to all comers. She *could* have resisted through genuine surliness; but this would put real feelings on show as much as would heart-felt cheeriness. Her resistance is cunning and she's in no mood to account for it to John, nor to deliver anything authentic to him. She preserves her authenticity by playing the role. John's solidarity is misplaced and inadvertently 'fingers' all this other stuff. She's annoyed enough to double-underline it with a '*you SHMUK!*'

Commercial trespass on heav'nly affairs

In one of 1998's late-summer editions, the *Daily Express* showed concern over the 'commercialisation of human feeling'. An Australian commercial radio station boosted its audience ratings and revenues by staging an unusual competition. The prize? A dream-come-true wedding with lavish reception and cash, on two conditions: first, that any would-be bride or groom entering the competition would be strangers to each other; second, that the one should propose to the other at the altar, immediately before the ceremony. A couple was duly matched. He proposed; she accepted. They were married on the spot. The groom's mother was dismayed. However the groom delighted in his bride, identified as one of the 'top 200' most beautiful women in town, declaring himself well on the way to 'falling in love'. The bride would only admit to making-a-go-of-it thus far.

This was a commercial intrusion into the emotional states of the listening audience, and of course into the lives of two young, perhaps more reckless than courageous individuals. The sacredness of weddings has been disturbed by the dollar, never mind that, in the first place, the dollar helped build the elaborate celebrations we see today - Stag Nights, Hen Nights and Happy Christmases. The dollar gives currency to feelings. It did not intrude. The dollar was us.

Forced to make heav'n's hellish struggle

The same edition of the *Express* protested against a US division of a supermarket chain, which insisted that their checkout operators work-up bright and familiar greetings for customers. Many customers were taken aback by the intensity of the welcome and this rebounded on worker and customer alike. Some men took the greetings as come-ons while, at the other tragic extreme, a worker had committed suicide. The *Express* protested at the strain placed on workers by insisting that they greet customers in this way, which they described as 'feigning' it.

The *Express* is saying that being *forced* to fabricate a Heaven is, in both cases, Hellish. Doubtless Milton lodged similar warnings against these kinds of commercial intrusions - one practised on a foolish bride and groom, with the fascinated public urging them on, the other on insecure workers who haven't the guile to resist. But again, what's special about emotional rather than mental or manual involvement?

Imagine the ease of organising a lightning strike at the checkout by passing the word. Look at the immediate impact: a riot of gleeful looting? If it was so bad at the checkout, this would have happened by now. Or would it? Are people so desperate for employment they'll feign cheery greetings at emotional cost to themselves.

Alienation compounded by damnation: Hochschild's *The Managed Heart*

What's wrong with putting yourself into the part, or being asked to do so? The use of words such as soul, heart and 'core of being', when discussing *self* and *emotion*, *head* and *mind* for *mental labour*, and *hands* and *body* for *manual labour*, points to something more than metaphor or tongue-in-cheek. Here's how a theology of emotion demarcates our Earthly parts from our otherworldly parts. Often there's a core and a periphery, with emotion placed centrally at this 'core of being' and manual labour at the periphery. Asked to map the body, most of my students place heart, soul and emotion together in the chest, separate from head, brain, mind, etc. Nasty emotions are placed in the viscera, and the nastiest in the guts or spleen, apparently still 'vented' from time to time. For many, this historically varying, far from universal map is just metaphorical. For others, it is practically the way it is. For some, the map shows that the commercialisation of emotion amounts to a metaphorical intrusion, seizing the heart/soul.

There's more than a passing resemblance between Hochschild's work and this theological concern with self - concern meaning 'focus of attention' and 'anxiety' or 'worrying'. A not-quite-accepted and not-quite-rejected theology informs Hochschild's concern.

Hochschild's evaluation of emotional labour has partly to do with *where emotions come from* (the heart) and with *the setting* (sacred or profane). Emotions are pictured either as *core* or as *elevated* above thought and our vaunted, otherworldly parts, because of the passions' sacred association with the heart/ as home to the soul.

Ignoring the *setting* for a moment, this association might result in an extremely positive evaluation of emotional labour as 'sacred/heart work' and 'above' mental and manual work.

But setting appears quite important for Hochschild. Her evaluation seems to turn on whether the work-setting is commercial or non-commercial, which implies that the object of labour is either *commodity* or *gift*. Hence: bad if heart felt *and* commercial, therefore intrusive (*Managed Heart*), good if heart felt *and* domestic; bad if emotional labour is absent at home (*Cold-Modern, Care-Deficit*); disturbing if there's a surplus of warmth at work (*Time Bind; When Work Becomes Home and Home Becomes Work*). She does not always say this, but I am fairly confident that a theology can be inferred. It's apparent enough in the title 'The Managed *Heart*, the *commercialisation* of *human* feeling', and, less clearly in her reference to the 'self which we *honour* as deep and integral to our individuality'.

Emotional labour for purely non-commercial good might be evaluated differently. If the setting is voluntary, domestic and sacred, the evaluation might be positive. The work of Samaritans, police bravery, NHS nursing, parent and child? It's only the materialist in Hochschild who insists on payment at the value of labour power, points out crises in over-production here, unsustainable 'speed-up' conditions there. It's the theologian who worries about what's being done to people's hearts, about soul-selling and soul-stealers.

What's the alternative? Most of the examples in this article suggest that we should probably tear up that metaphorical map of the body and its treasured regions, and therefore not worry about commercial trespass on places marked 'soul' and 'heart' - there are no such places. We should welcome unaffected emotional labour wherever it is found - among commercial workers (the ex-nursing sales worker) and when freely given (the colleague). We should see it as no different from mental or manual skilfulness - placing the craft worker firmly in charge of their labours, public or private. We should be forgiving when the emotional labourer chooses to withhold (John's checkout encounter and my visit to the rock and roll review) - perhaps because the map remains vital to them, or because they are wary of the demands of employers (and guests), or because they are best placed to know their own capacity to do emotional labour. One thing is certain - having accepted the stuff of emotional labour a 'Day in the Life' will never be quite the same again.

The immigrant experience

Affective and effective spheres and issues of race and gender

Minoo Moallem

Through looking at the working experiences of migrant workers, Minoo Moallem examines the porous borders between work and home, and between the public and private spheres, particularly in relation to emotional labour.

In this essay, through looking at the experiences of Iranian immigrant entrepreneurs, I aim to illuminate some of the ways in which the separation of the effective and affective spheres operates as an important component of the split between public and private, market and home, and state and civil society. In each of these splits the performance of work versus care is allocated to one side of the divide, in a way that legitimises existing sexual and racial divisions of labour. In addition, political citizenship is split off from any ethic of care (defined by relationships and interconnectedness), and instead is based on an ethic of responsibility (defined by abstract and imaginary notions of community). The disjunction of the affective and the effective is central to a notion of citizenship which separates the political sphere from civil society, and contributes to the naturalisation and normalisation of caring as 'non-work'. It also fosters the separation of bodies from their work, promoting a disembodied citizenship. Feminist critiques of a political economy based on the separation of domestic and non-domestic spheres - one assigned to economically useful work and the other to non-work - and analyses of the increasing feminisation of the labour market have made very important contributions to our understanding of the feminisation of space and its consequences for women's lives. The concentration of women and racialised groups in the feminised, ethnicised and secondary segments of the market (characterised as low-paid, dead-end, labour intensive, with a high reliance on service and caring) has been an important focus for feminist and anti-racist critiques of the gender and racial division of labour. With the increase in globalisation and the expansion of flexibility and the subcontracting of labour, these sexual and racial patterns are taking new forms. As a consequence, the domestic and the non-domestic are merging, to maximise flexibility while minimising costs and risks. The 'home' is increasingly becoming a privileged site of flexible capital and labour that provides the effective incorporation of labour intensive work into the market. But at the same time the feminised and racialised segments of the market rely heavily on the affective relations of home for survival or success, leading to the packaging of care as 'excess of work'. Small immigrant entrepreneurial activities provide a rich field in which to study the impact of these changes.

Immigrant entrepreneurs as caregivers

Ethnic entrepreneurial spaces are now a familiar part of public spaces in which effective modes of economic activity are linked to affective modes of being. They are contrived by national boundaries and increasingly transnational cultural and economic networks. Furthermore, they are the most visible spaces in which cultural difference is expressed through economic activity.

Iranians are among the new immigrants who have found spaces of hope and continuity in small businesses. While some entrepreneurs find a place in existing categories of business activities, others base their businesses on their distinct cultural identity. Familiar icons from the travelling memories of migrants inform the process of naming, and invest certain products and their consumption with symbolic, affective values. In the interplay of culture and economics, and through the performance of the economic actions of everyday life, cultural goods and meanings move around, blurring the boundaries between the symbolic demands of cultural difference and the economic demands of everyday survival. The presence of Zafran rice on the menus of Italian restaurants in San Francisco, of 'Isfahan' in the middle of Paris, or of 'Khayam' in Berlin does not have much to do with certain naive notions of multiculturalism, but demonstrates the insistence of the diasporic presence and the impossibility of its effacement and suppression from the dominant material and symbolic infrastructures. The links between social memory, space, migrancy and economics in the discourses and practices of immigrants are part and parcel of new forms of global restructuring and transnationalism.

Blending of the affective and the effective in Parvin's snack bar

For immigrants, many entrepreneurial spaces are spaces of social and community care. For example, Parvin has a small snack bar in a shopping mall in Berlin. She is from an upper-middle-class background, and opened her business only after experiencing great difficulty finding a job in her profession:

> My kids cannot believe that I had servants and nannies and even a driver in Iran. Here in Germany, I have been treated like nobody. Even to start a business, you need so many permits, you have to deal with so many bureaucrats who treat you so badly, you have to prove to so many institutions that you can make it, running from one inspection to another, and you are constantly treated with a lot of suspicion and distrust.

Her class, gender and family resources (her husband and her children are involved in the snack bar), as well as a one-year training in small entrepreneurship offered by *Initiative selbständiger Immigrantinnen*, have been crucial in enabling her to start a business. However, she has been forced to give up any clear identification between her business and her Iranian culture because of racist reactions:

> When I opened this place, I put up a sign advertising Persian specialities. But I heard people talking about Khomeini and Salman Rushdie. Many looked at me in a strange way. I was not getting enough clients, and at this location I mainly rely on German clients. I could not afford to lose them. Once, a couple

passed by and the woman suggested that they have a cappuccino, but the man refused. In a very loud voice, he said, 'I do not drink a foreigner's cappuccino', so I changed my sign.

But Parvin has not given up her affective connections to Iranian culture. She has effectively incorporated them into her business activities. One way of doing this is by cooking Iranian dishes and presenting them under a German name.

I have managed to put some Iranian food on the menu, but I have given it different names. [She laughs.] This *Genussesnack*, for example, is nothing but our own *Kou Kou Sabzi*. The same with the eggplant dish. They don't want to identify these dishes with my culture, but that doesn't make any difference to me. I get to have them on the menu because they are special to me.

For Parvin, another opportunity to blend the affective and the effective is her work of 'caring'. She combines her abilities and knowledge as a former social worker, her Iranian cultural notions of hospitality, and her gender position as a wife, mother and older sister in her small business:

This is a highly individualistic society. People need attention and care. I use Iranian hospitality to comfort them here. I talk to them, I pay attention to what they tell me, I give them suggestions about what to do and what not to do. At the end of the day, I even give up my extra bread and croissants - I ask my clients if they want to take some home. Sometimes, I make Persian cookies and leave them here for everyone. In this way, I have been able to create a stable clientele. They might try other places once in a while, but they always come back to me.

Parvin organises the daily rituals of business interactions so that there is no separation between her affective relationship with her culture and her effective methods of doing business in a hostile environment. Caring as feminised and invisible work - identified increasingly with an immigrant and ethnic division of labour - manifests itself in her entrepreneurial strategies of survival and success. Through the discursive boundaries of foreignness and belonging, the German market is able to exploit the unpaid work of caring performed by Parvin in her daily business interactions, and she is able to offer it voluntarily as a natural part of her business activities.

What is 'homey' in Taghi's Café?

Taghi is an Iranian businessman in Berlin whose entrepreneurial activities rely extensively on his work of caring. In his case, caring is directed toward community members. Taghi has a hybrid shop in Berlin: his business is divided between a small Persian finger-food counter at the front and a travel agency at the back. There is no door between the two sections, but one does not immediately notice the desk, computer and fax machine in the rear. The walls of the store are covered with pictures of Iranian monuments and cities. I am received kindly, and treated to tea and fresh fruit. I sit with Taghi and we start talking. There are some Iranian men sitting outside, playing chess and backgammon. During the interview, I see both women and men dropping by for different reasons. The café has a homey atmosphere; people come and go. Since Taghi and another Iranian who works for him are from Azerbaijan, one hears Farsi and Turkish being spoken in the store. Occasionally, a German-speaking client walks in and is addressed in German. Phones ring constantly. Taghi tells me that he has a phone line connected to several Iranian homes where kids are left alone by working parents and instructed to call Taghi if they have any problems.

> I don't charge them for this service. I try to be helpful. They make sure that their kids have access to someone from the community, and it is not much work for us. Sometimes the kids just call and talk to us and get support until their parents are back home.

Taghi studied engineering in Germany and had also been active on the Iranian left. His migration resulted from the political repression of the left by the Islamic Republic. After migrating to Germany, Taghi obtained a teaching job at a university and stayed there for a few years, but when it became clear that he was unlikely to find a permanent position in his profession, he too turned to business:

> Many Germans think that we are taking their places. They don't know how much hassle we have to go through to make a living. I come from an academic and activist background, but I have learned to cook, to talk to all these small business bureaucrats, and to use day-to-day business language, etc. People see us working, but never ask how we've managed to survive.

In his business, Taghi is not only trying to create a space where Iranians feel at home and can come and ask for different services. He also organises cultural activities, lectures and exhibitions.

> Some people come here to talk to me about their problems, some come to meet with others, and some come to get information about different activities in the community. I have notices about all kinds of cultural activities.

Taghi is no longer involved with political activism, but he remains very concerned about the well-being of Iranian exiles. His concerns have turned towards the care of community members and the development of an effective mode of entrepreneurship. In his business, politics, economics and culture merge, spanning the gulf between Germany and Iran and connecting also with other diasporic locations. His work of caring brings its rewards: he has been able to add his travel agency to his finger-food store because of the effective and affective connections that he has established between his entrepreneurial activities and community needs.

> I started to expand my business and opened a travel agency when I saw so many people around me who trusted me. I have been successful because I am able to serve them almost 24 hours a day. Some of my clients have very little time and come and see me late at night. Some prefer to deal in Farsi and trust me to find them good deals. These days, many Iranians travel back and forth to Iran and to other parts of the world where they have family. The presence of a considerable number of Iranians in diaspora has created a market for a travel agent who can serve them conveniently. In addition, I perform extra services such as sending medications or gifts with travellers. Sometimes people need to send a power of attorney, a legal document or simply urgent messages. I always do my best to be helpful to them.

Taghi's business is more than an entrepreneurial space. It is an affective community space. Here, culture and economics meet and enrich each other through the creation of some sense of control and power. It is also a transnational space where Iran and Berlin are experienced through social interactions which blend national and ethnic boundaries.

As foreigners, we need to have our own spaces where we can take care of each other. I personally get a lot of energy from this business and the kind of life I have here. It gives me hope, as well as a sense of continuity and connection. When I see my fellow Iranians milling around and talking to each other, I feel very happy and joyous. For me, this is a business and also more than a business.

Beside citizenship

Small entrepreneurial spaces are quintessential examples of those transnational spaces where notions of time and space are blurred and transgressed in a number of different ways. First of all, these spaces challenge a linear notion of time and space, expressed in the dichotomy between here and there, homeland and host society, third world and first world, as well as home and market. Secondly, for massive groups of immigrants, the production and consumption of 'cultural goods' and the specialisation in small businesses do not arise solely from the collectivity's decision to preserve its common memories; a bigger factor is that, in the context of a daily experience of restriction and discrimination, ethnic entrepreneurial activities create an economic continuity that opens up the possibility of employment, money and hope in diaspora. Thirdly, with the expansion of new forms of globalisation and the presence of diasporic people in different locations and territories, new transnational entrepreneurial possibilities are emerging, and cultural boundaries are being realigned. Immigrant entrepreneurs are becoming new economic agents, facilitating the movement of capital, labour and culture from one location to another, from the private to the public sphere and from the formal to the informal, or *vice versa*. Their existence challenges modern politico-spatial divisions based on national territoriality and market-centred economism. The entrepreneurial presence of immigrants also challenges any narrow conception of participation in a centralised, state-regulated politics, placing in crisis the narrow confines of both modern nationalism and the global city-state. In this context, ethnic entrepreneurial spaces can be characterised as spaces of everyday self-government, where past and present, there and here, outside and inside, affective and effective, encounter each other.

These case studies demonstrate how the everyday life practices of immigrants are articulated inside, between and beyond the boundaries of culture and economy, care and work, here and there, home and market, and point to new spaces of be/longing and citizenship.

Beyond the wall

Changing political cultures of the informal sphere

Prue Chamberlayne

Prue Chamberlayne *reflects on the - sometimes surprising - discoveries made in a recent research programme looking at different cultures of care in Britain and in Germany, East and West.*

Those lurching mirrors which sometimes stand at driveway junctions and awkward corners can be disconcerting: is one seeing the road one just came along or the one ahead? Comparative analysis similarly faces two ways, often as intriguing in its reflections on one's own society as of the one under review. This has been my experience in conducting research into informal 'cultures of care' in East and West Germany, which threw into relief not just differences between those two culturally polarised societies, but some particularities of British patterns of caring.

The research was concerned with the informal social contexts in which caring is situated in different societies, contexts which give rise to different characteristic strategies, in terms of preparedness to mobilise outside as opposed to family or personal resources, and different degrees of confidence and competence to challenge official diagnoses and decisions. While not directly concerned with emotions of caring, the research implies different emotional worlds at the interface of everyday life and welfare systems, and different cultures of support, between partners, within families and informal networks, and between

167

carers and various kinds of professionals. There is no question but that caring involves emotion - much of it in furious struggles for resources and services, and against the constraining effects of situations of caring and disability.

Caring is situated in the interstices of public and private worlds, structured by personal and family dynamics, by welfare systems, and by wider cultural and social patterns. Caring situations are thus likely to vary significantly both between and within different societies. Yet within the framework of social policy, the dynamics of the informal sphere remain extraordinarily opaque. Feminism has succeeded in prising open many aspects of 'private' home life to social analysis, although the adjacent sphere of 'the social', in which, it has been argued, women are 'enmeshed', remains unexamined, even unrecognised. In social policy's cognate discipline of political science, the informal social sphere remains 'private', 'beneath' the boundaries of civil society, and positivistic Fabianism has always been interested in designs from above rather than strategies and resources from below. With the formation of the Labour Party, Fabianism played no mean role in the statisation of mutual and friendly society traditions, that rich infrastructure in the social sphere. Fortunately, the Europeanisation of welfare enlarges our conceptual and practical repertoires and Anglo-Saxon social policy's lack of a language for thinking about dynamics in the informal sphere is already being challenged by the new emphasis on 'social capital' and 'strengthening the social', concepts which are stronger in Continental and especially Catholic thinking.

Neither is the turn within social theory by writers such as Giddens and Beck to gender equality and personal intimacy much help to a study of caring in the informal sphere. Unlike feminist theory and the new social movements, their thinking ignores the impact of either relational dependencies or domestic labour on identities. This implicitly leaves carers as Cinderellas of modernity, excluded from the emancipatory effects of either employment or autonomous personal lives, excluded also from the analysis. It also accords with the insistence in Marxist theory on employment as the key to women's public involvement, and the consequent neglect of social and historical variations in forms of engagement between household activities and the outside world. By contrast, Laura Balbo, writing within the context of developed welfare systems, argues that women's roles in mediating and negotiating relationships between family members and with outside agencies generate 'modern' skills, 'catapulting' women from the periphery to the centre of society. And indeed, changes in the balancing of public and private roles and resources may for many sections of contemporary society be a key feature of shifts towards post- or late modernity.

In all three societies in the Cultures of Care study there were carers who became more domestically confined by caring and those whose strategies drew them into more active involvement with the outside world.[1] Those who became more home-oriented tended to become stuck in the present, losing hold of either past identities or future horizons, whereas carers who were more vigorously involved with outside agencies and networks were more proactive in adapting to change in the caring situation, and able to retain a sense of self and identity beyond caring. There was a generational pattern, with younger carers in all three societies more likely to be more outgoing, and older carers more likely to adopt the 'home fortress' strategy.

While a similar spread of home- and outward- orientedness appeared in each society, the characteristic dynamic arising from the interplay of personal factors/family pressures, informal networks and service contexts was markedly different in each society. These patterns of engagement with the private and public spheres in some senses followed, but in important ways contradicted, official policy norms. This suggests that the lived experience of welfare situations is structured by social and cultural dynamics which lie beyond the frame of reference of social policy.

◆ In West Germany, where subsidiarity's traditional encouragement of community and family, and its more recent stress on self-help initiatives, would lead one to expect a supportive communal life, carers seemed *least* likely to be drawn out of domestic isolation.

◆ East Germany, whose regime disavowed the very concept of 'civil society', gave rise to the most active informal engagement.

◆ Despite its voluntary tradition and relatively strong web of communal relationships, Britain seemed to lead carers, following energetic but eventually disappointing forays into the social world, to fall back on their own personal and family resources.

---

1. The research was based on biographical interviews with twenty unpaid family carers in each of three cities (Bremen, Leipzig and London). The interviews were conducted in 1992 in East and West Germany and in 1995 in Britain.

The key factors which contributed to these characteristic dynamics were of a very different order in each society. Their 'opposite' nature in West and East Germany supports arguments concerning the structural and cultural incompatibilities of the 'two Germanys', and of the unlikely effectiveness of transplanting West German administrative systems into such a different social terrain. The extent of the differences, given the historically short-lived existence (40 years) of state socialism in East Germany, also bears witness to the extent to which social and cultural change *can* be engineered.

Formal social policy exerted opposite dynamics in the two Germanys. In West Germany carers were 'pulled into' the home by the emphasis on domiciliary services, a traditional sense of personal vocation in the domestic sphere and continuation of 'housewife' roles, together with a housing design tradition of sizeable, often self-built, family homes. In East Germany they were 'pushed out' of the home by traditions of full employment for women, the organisation of collective services outside the home, and the small size of dwellings. And within these counterposed structures, opposite ideologies of the family, social values and informal cultures exerted further pressure towards contrasting responses in caring situations.

In both societies support from sympathetic professionals was often critical in gaining the confidence to challenge officialdom. In West Germany such contact was likely to come from lower level professionals like physiotherapists or specialist nurses or psychologists who might make regular home visits, and sometimes from community workers, and the issues concerned diagnoses and treatments, together with benefit entitlements. In East Germany the carers were more likely to seek out their own contacts and information through wide ranging networks, often involving people not originally known to them.

The contradictory nature of cultural forms stands out in each case. In West Germany the 'perversity' of such forms lies in the continuing hold of traditional family ideologies, beyond the intentions of policy makers. In European discourse, subsidiarity is taken to mean downward delegation of responsibility to church and other voluntary welfare organisations and to self-help initiatives. It also includes the maximising of family responsibility, and the West German cases show the force of that ideology, especially among older carers, but perhaps by a 'tyrannical' older mother, and perhaps by other family members.

One carer, aged 50, felt that all her life had been cast in the role of family helper in her parents' grocery: 'caring was laid with me in my cradle'. Still struggling against her subordination to her mother, she eventually and ingeniously managed to pursue her craft and music interests as hobbies, but still without being able to persuade her mother to accept more 'outside' domiciliary services, even though these were being insistently offered. Another carer, aged 60, who liked 'to do things properly', insisted on bringing her terminally ill husband home, where she railed against the failure of wider family members to give the kind of support she and her sisters had devoted to their parents. The same pattern arose in a much younger woman, aged 35, a medical high-flier, who had fallen in love with a married dentist. Having had a disabled child, she found herself isolated and trapped in his family practice, regarded by his hostile family as 'the perfect carer', given her medical skills.

Although the 'strong breadwinner' model of West German welfare does privilege traditional family forms, the deleterious consequences of 'family responsibility' devolving on an unaided wife, daughter or mother has long been recognised in policy and professional training. Yet extreme versions are being lived out in caring, as the examples show. Carers in our study who 'escaped' the traditional family hierarchies and divisions of class, generation, gender and 'privacy' which characterised the West German model were from more marginalised or skeletal families, associated with 'alternative' cultures, and aided by partners in caring tasks. (It should be noted that a different location, and especially Berlin, might have yielded a stronger representation of carers from 'alternative' milieus.)

The networks of the few more outwardly-oriented West German carers in the study and the generality of East German cases, were characterised by horizontality, flexibility and trust, recalling the features of 'civic competence' as defined in Putnam's study of co-operative relationships in Northern Italy.[2] The strength of informal networks in East Germany was by no means officially intended, but resulted from inadequacies in the service sector. It may well be that the repression of civil society in East Germany pushed active social engagement down to informal levels, such as 'work' and 'house collectives', where a need for human communication spilled out regardless of official attempts at surveillance. The 'social levelling' within East Germany also facilitated the exchange of social advice. It

---

2. D. Putnam, *Making Democracy Work: Civic Traditions in Modern Italy*, Princeton University Press 1993.

has been argued that humanist values of equality and participation permeated East German society, and that Party claims to socialist superiority in satisfying human needs fuelled a rights-consciousness in the population, and enraged those most dependent on welfare services. In addition, party organisation was centred on the workplace, leaving public and neighbourhood services somewhat more free. Shared understandings among elderly and disabled people of the failures and hypocrisies of the system amounted to a 'quiet social movement', which then burst into the public sphere in 1989 and 1990.

For East German carers, therefore, who like carers anywhere were involved in life and death struggles against medical callousness and false diagnoses, and needed to obtain adequate and tailor-made services for highly particularised conditions, there existed already in the culture of everyday life usable channels of communication and support, and a propulsion to seek solutions outside the home. One single parent carer, aged 23, originally a canteen worker, seemed trapped at the time of the first interview by the assistance of her patriarchal family, who had taken her into their home on weekdays so that they could take the child to the crèche, while she retrained for a secure public service job. Her father's mission was to save his daughter (and the family) from becoming 'a social case, one which would stay in the records'. But at the weekends she stayed at her own flat on an outlying estate, where she was part of a group of parents of disabled children, which had been established by a social worker. Through her contacts with a dynamic mental disability group, this rather meagrely qualified young woman procured an early operation by a specialist doctor, legal help in fighting her benefit reduction, and access to an integrated crèche and then kindergarten. By the second interview she had returned to the estate.

Another older woman, aged 60, whose husband's severe stroke had coincided with his lay-off as a transport engineer, likewise sallied forth in combat and determination for improved services, helped by networks of information, a rights-conscious culture, and anger, not least at the 'dangers' of unification. This woman, helped in fighting bureaucracy by a career in supplies for the textile industry, is nevertheless also engaged in a struggle against an internalised family tradition of female caring and her subordinate role in the marriage:

Frau Blau: (Pause) Through this I have become much more independent, more independent than ...

Herr Blau: You were like this before.

Frau Blau: But not like this, Hans-Otto. I have to represent us completely to the outside world … (pause) and I have to check myself sometimes, because I am out there alone, but I am still (saying) 'we' …

The contrast between this energetic and outgoing woman and her more defeated West German counterparts who were mentioned above is striking.

The cultural effects of policy measures are also highlighted in the area of disability. In West Germany, since disability payments rose with the severity of the disability, the impulse was to exaggerate the condition, and seek medical and even legal support to prove its severity. In East Germany the pressure was to underrate the severity, since relatively able young disabled people received education, training, and guaranteed workplaces with salaries, whereas those considered 'incapable of development' (*foerderunfaehig*) were consigned to residential warehousing. The heroic tirelessness of many East German parents in seeking out integrated forms of schooling, acquiring equipment and themselves training in and conducting physical therapies was in part stimulated by this politics of disability.

The British carers in the study had for many years combined caring, employment and wider voluntary and social activity. The dominant cultural dynamic was nevertheless towards home solutions, although the routes by which British and West German carers found themselves centred in the private sphere were different. Outside social engagement through part-time work, day centres, respite care, voluntary and self-help groups, together with help in caring tasks from husbands, existed in greater measure than in West Germany. But welfare cutbacks and fragmentation in the 1980s and 1990s had turned carers back on their own resources and family tradition, even those from which they have previously escaped. This intensified intergenerational dependencies, especially in late adolescence in the void between education and adult services, which made it very difficult for parents to move positively towards officially espoused 'independent living'.

Mrs Buckley, aged 55, was emblematic of these processes. Coming from a large Catholic East End family, she initially defied her family's prolonged child-bearing norms through a successful and mobile career. On giving birth to a disabled daughter in her 30s she started on a long career of struggles for appropriate referrals, and despite repeated health crises in which she stopped work, she valiantly regained employment. She was actively supported in this by medical personnel at a specialist children's hospital, and she continued her involvement in voluntary groups. In her daughter's late teens, however, in the shift from education to adult services, and in the context of the cost-cutting 1990s, there was no such support, and reduced day centre schedules became difficult to reconcile with employment. Moreover circumstances occurred which excluded Mr Buckley from the direct caring role he used to play. A friend's car accident was the final straw for Mrs Buckley:

> I was so upset about that and I thought, 'Oh I'll pack up work'. I did it on the spur of the moment … I did feel a bit, not bitter towards her, but I just feel sometimes, 'Oh, why did I have to pack up my job, because I liked it'.

Now there seemed to be a service void, in a period in which Mrs Buckley needed active and positive support to find good alternatives for Melanie.

We had expected that the greater 'politicisation' of caring in Britain as compared with West or East Germany might have bolstered outward-orientedness.[3] In fact the carers' groups seemed to operate more as an extension of the private sphere - providing solace, 'a laugh' and basic information - than as a bridgehead to wider contacts or to more transformative action, whether individually or collectively. This confirmed the thesis that carers' groups in Britain have become 'incorporated', in contrast with disability groups, which have maintained the momentum of a social movement. Maybe, as in West Germany, it is the pull of traditional family ideology which acts as such a conservatising force in caring, whereas the disability movement is more oriented to peer group networks. Age clearly plays a role too, since in general younger carers were more outgoing.

The fact that carers' groups in Britain and 'self-help' groups in West Germany are held up as an example of 'empowerment' relativises the meaning of the term. In either context the main function of carers' groups (though there were few in Germany) seems to be the maintaining of inadequately serviced situations (the

---

3. Although throughout the 1990s discussions and legislation concerning the new 'care insurance' (*Pflegeversicherung*) has made caring a highly political issue in Germany - but not in the form which has involved political actions by carers themselves.

'caring deficit' in Arlie Hochschild's terms[4]), together with combating a defeatism which is service-induced. Both welfare systems are faced with the need to remedy a social incapacity which is of the system's own making, whereas in different structural and cultural conditions there might be no need for such 'empowerment'. This much is made clear by the East German example, where 'empowerment' is derived from wider social infrastructures, such as the full employment model for women, an egalitarian ethos, and the strength of informal networks.

It is not being argued that the East German situation should be replicated elsewhere, but it is important to identify some of the wider determinants and components of a more energised and supportive culture in the informal sphere.

Conclusion

The Cultures of Care study highlights the social vibrancy and creativity which accompanies more outward-oriented forms of caring. In them we also see the potential for equality between carers and professionals, through the gaining of social competence and recognition among lay experts. The need for a different relationship between social lives and welfare services is also made clear, one which will strengthen human relatedness and operate in a context of trust. The study suggests that where social trust and 'the social' are denser and social capital is richer,' can become more resourceful in seeking out tailor-made support. And that it is wider social relations which give rise to particular imagined worlds in which such actions are possible and indeed socially engendered - or foreclosed on. Sensitivity to such 'social relations' goes well beyond the usual parameters of social policy, which tends to operate with 'thin' knowledge of social systems. This study suggests the need for more culturally and sociologically specified accounts of informal social situations and contexts.

This article owes much to Annette King, who was the main researcher for the Cultures of Care project, which was ESRC funded in 1992-5. Frauke Ruppel, Susanne Rupp and Chris King also worked as researchers on the British part of the project which was funded by the UEL 1995-7. A fuller version will appear in P. Chamberlayne, A.Cooper and R Freeman (eds), Welfare and Culture, Jessica Kingsley 1999. Thanks to Andrew Cooper and Jude Bloomfield for comments.

---

4. A. R. Hochschild, 'The Culture of Politics: Traditional, Postmodern, Cold-modern, and warm-modern ideals of care', *Social Politics*, Fall 1995.

New mournings?

Photo-essay by Rosy Martin

Rosy Martin's pictures are an attempt to represent the emotional and psychic work that an individual does in coming to terms with bereavement. This work was made as part of her grieving and reparation after the death of her father, and of Jo Spence, the artist with whom Rosy Martin collaborated

In grief and loss my abandoned child-self returns, takes centre stage in her terror, desolation and powerlessness.

Her cry 'take care of me, love me whatever, accept as I am, don't leave me.'

Into a deep, dark hole, spiralling out of control, soft warm tears unbidden flow, my mind unfocused, my heart hurting. 'Help me, help me', but neither she nor he can any longer hear. No longer here. Only death, only decay, only finality. My despair: that there is no return to my imagined Eden, to my sweet illusions. Lost. In the pain of loss I find what it was I truly valued in each, specific loss.

I inhabit again and again that child who never grows and learn more each time I touch my vulnerability. It is as if to change we must keep in touch with the changeless.

There is, too, a nurturing, caring part of me, so ready to listen to the pain of others. My needy helper, she gives what she needs to receive. She hears the cry, can she learn to respond? Slowly and unsure at first she contains and holds. Can I learn to take care of my own needy child-self?

Embrace life. The part of me who reaches out for new possibilities, brave and courageous in the face of loss and rejection. Learning to let go, she finds the strength to begin to move old obstacles, to recognise new blooms. The phoenix, with singed wings, must learn to fly again. Coming out of the shadow, yet part of the shadow: in death, life, in life death.

Student carers

Learning to manage emotions

Sue Williams

Sue Williams *looks at the role of emotional labour in the training of student nurses.*

This article aims to highlight some of issues which surround the concept of emotional labour within nursing, from an educational perspective.

Since the introduction of the Project 2000 style of training, student nurses have been actively encouraged to identify and develop skills which will enable them to communicate with sensitivity, and to reflect with insight upon those interactions which they themselves perceive as meaningful. These interactions, and the emotional relationships upon which they are often founded, can become the catalyst for expanding self-awareness. Self awareness has been defined as the gradual process of noticing and exploring aspects of self, and it is seen as an essential skill for reflection.[1] However strategies of reflection and reflective practice have been accepted within the nursing profession relatively uncritically and may be fundamentally flawed.[2] It has been suggested that the majority of student nurses may be unable to reflect on their practice in any way other than purely superficially. Another reason for concern - at both the use of reflection and the associated emphasis on promoting self awareness for students within an educational setting - is the need for skilled facilitation by teachers managing this activity.

---

1. Burnard and Morrison, *Caring and Communicating. The Interpersonal Relationship in Nursing,* Macmillan, London 1991.
2. C. Mackintosh, 'Reflection: a flawed strategy for the nursing profession', *Nurse Education Today* 18, pp553 – 557, 1998.

Two scenarios will be described in this article, which have been taken from separate teaching sessions. On both occasions the reflection seemed to touch on issues deeper than the merely superficial level. In the first example an invitation to discuss a clinical issue, within a receptive small group, seemed to give an opportunity for enhanced self-awareness to take place. In the second example the use of a specific exercise aimed at increasing self-awareness created an opportunity for emotional catharsis which also required sensitive facilitation. Situations such as these, when there is sufficient space to disclose and reflect upon personal material, can be very powerful in their potential to increase insight for the student, but must take place within an environment which maximises psychological safety for those concerned.

I feel sure that taking the opportunity to help the student become more aware of emotional issues surrounding the care of patients has great value for the student, but, equally importantly, it has value for the patient, both present and future. The need for nurses to be 'in touch' with their feelings was emphasised by Benner, who felt that among the characteristics of an expert nurse was included the ability to listen to their feelings, for example when making clinical judgements.[3] These feelings may be understood to be something concerning the patient as an individual, or may be perceived by the nurse as an internal experience of emotional discomfort which she is unable to understand. The activity of nursing the patient can act as a trigger which reactivates feelings related to past events which she is unable to attach to any readily accessible memories of her own. When this occurs, particularly for the relatively inexperienced student nurse, the result may be overwhelming anxiety. Therefore it can be of value to enable the student to make connections between past and present events, so enabling her to gain further understanding and take control of her present.

Memories may be thought to be 'lost' to conscious recollection for various reasons, including a process of repression as described by classic psychoanalytic theory. However, as can be seen by debates concerning the creation of false memory syndrome within some styles of psychotherapy, there can be considerable ethical difficulties in using techniques which focus on retrieving such memories, especially within a setting which has

---

3. P. Benner, *From Novice to Expert*, Addison-Wesley, New York 1984.

an educational rather than a therapeutic agenda.[4]

On the other hand, experiences may be remembered as factual events but become divorced from felt emotions: recall without affect produces no emotional catharsis, however distressing the memory is thought to be by the individual. This was seen clearly in the first scenario described here, which involves students reflecting upon their recent paediatric placement.

One member of the group was a mature woman who had two children at senior school, who had needed to show a high degree of commitment to gain the necessary qualifications to undertake nurse training. When hearing students in the group talk about their paediatric placement she looked somewhat uneasy, and several of her friends encouraged her to speak of her experience. She spoke in a soft, shaking voice quite unlike her usual assertive tone, and at times she was close to tears. She recounted how a young girl of twelve months had been admitted to the ward for investigation of a blood disorder. She rarely had visitors as her mother had just given birth to another child and the student felt the family were neglecting her in order to concentrate on the new baby. Much to the student's horror, she found herself becoming increasingly preoccupied by her young patient, for example worrying that the staff were not paying her enough attention when she herself was off duty, and bringing her small toys. She also reported having nightmares where the child was crying and she was unable to respond because of feeling totally 'helpless'. She thought her response to the child was 'irrational', and, as she didn't understand why she was feeling so out of control of her emotions, she felt that her future career in nursing was uncertain. She was unable to seek help from trained staff as she felt ashamed of her feelings, and on those occasions when trained staff noticed her growing preoccupation with the child they always took a very rational, concrete approach, on the lines of 'a good nurse cares for *all* her patients equally', and 'a good nurse *never* becomes over involved with her patients'. These well meaning comments only reinforced her own conclusions that she was somehow failing to be a 'good enough' nurse.

While listening to her speak I felt that she was struggling to understand what for her was an overwhelmingly emotional experience, while using only

---

4. P. Mollon, 'False memories; finding a balance', *Advances in Psychiatric Treatment*, Vol. 4, Royal College of Psychiatrists 1998.

rationalistic concepts. The situation seemed to be one involving a child with whom the student was strongly identifying: many of the words she used mirrored this theme, such as feeling 'helpless' and 'out of control'; and other aspects of her communication, such as her soft, shaking voice, reinforced this idea.

I asked her if she had ever been in hospital herself, and she spoke of having her two children in hospital. She fell silent and I observed that having that experience as an adult in hospital must feel very different from being a child in hospital. All again fell silent as she appeared to be thinking intently. She then said, 'yes it did feel different', and then, after a short pause, she said 'I was in hospital when I was three but I can't really remember much about it - I know I had been scalded and given skin grafts on my chest because I still have the scars'.

> 'She was struggling to understand an overwhelmingly emotional experience, using only rationalistic concepts'

Several members of the group leaned forward looking very interested, and one of them, who seemed to know her well, said 'you've never mentioned this before'. The student replied, 'It was years ago. I know it happened but I can't remember ever feeling upset by it so I had no reason to talk about it - actually I don't think I've even told my husband'.

I commented that, although what happened may rationally belong in the past, perhaps her intensely emotional response to her patient was giving her an alternative message. She said, 'Do you think the way I've been feeling is about me not her?' I answered that she seemed to have tried very hard to give good emotional care to her patient, and perhaps in the process past needs of her own had surfaced and become mixed up with what was happening in the here and now.

The session continued with group members offering their perceptions. At the close it was felt that nursing can trigger emotions that may be more to do with past than present events. The student who had initially spoken in the group felt that, in retrospect, what had made it difficult for her to ask for help was a sense that what was happening to her was totally alien; in fact what had happened, due to this group experience, was that for the first time she was able to think of her emotional responses to the child as perfectly understandable when viewed in the context of her past experiences. Her relief at being able to normalise her feelings, and thus to view her future placements as challenging but not as potentially devastating emotional minefields was obvious, both in her verbal responses and non-verbally - she was now speaking in her usual confident and animated way.

The second scenario I want to describe occurred within a somewhat different group, involving students in the final year of a programme of study leading to a qualification in mental health nursing. The setting was also different as this group was used to working together on a regular basis, and had experienced a variety of projective group techniques facilitated by each of the group members in pairs, in turn. This particular session was facilitated by myself and a colleague using collage as a medium for self-expression. The session involved each group member contributing a range of magazines. This collection of material was torn into single pages and heaped into a pile in the centre of the room. Participants were encouraged to get on the floor and immerse themselves in the images, and then collect those pictures which told the group something about themselves, finally using these to form a collage. The room was then rearranged so that all evidence of the exercise was removed, leaving only a circle of seats and the finished collages.

In the group that followed each individual spoke of their collage and the personal relevance of the chosen images. A male student in his late twenties had a picture one section of which was composed entirely of female breasts unattached to any other part of the body. He told the group that he was a 'bit of a boob man', and the group responded in a similarly light-hearted way. Although the group had no interpretative function, I felt that it might be helpful to model a question based on a hunch, which he could choose to respond to or not. I asked him if his mother was still alive, and when he answered in the affirmative I said 'Could you describe her?' He sat very silent and still for a moment, then said, 'Do you mean how she looked when I was a child?' He had taken my question in this direction, so I answered 'if you can'. The group had quickly become hushed and there was a feeling of tension. The student said 'I cannot remember her face then, I lost her when I was three'. We waited and he said. 'My father came and took me away from her'.

The atmosphere in the group had changed so quickly that some students were looking confused; others were leaning forward expectantly. Rather than asking concrete questions about the circumstances of the separation I chose to stay with the emotional content of his disclosure. I asked how he felt remembering what happened. After a short silence, in which he was rapidly blinking back tears, he said, 'I had to be brave, my father came and took me because it was time to learn how to be a man'. I observed that it must have been difficult to 'be a man', when he must have felt like crying. He nodded and some tears rolled down his face. The group waited and after a minute he began to 'tell us his story', especially in relation to the special cultural factors which provided a context in which his story was heard. As he spoke there was a noticeable reduction in anxiety and distress both for the student and for the group as a whole.

Josephine Klein describes how talking puts experiences into words; sometimes talking allows us to connect experiences with words for the first time.[5] As we 'give an account' of those experiences we again become aware of their emotional impact. Once these experiences are fully conscious and the individual has taken on the role of narrator, we see a helpful aspect of the process of depersonalising and distancing. The 'I then' and the 'I now' are separated in time, and this distance allows for a new perspective and a new meaning. What is important in the incident that I am describing is that sufficient psychological safety was offered to enable the student to feel that what happened 'then', when he was small and weak, cannot threaten him now - that he the adult can hold this memory of he as the frightened child, process it, and allow it to be reintegrated into the adult personality.

Both of the scenarios described here are only 'snapshots' taken from what were longer and more involved group experiences, but I have chosen them as examples of the kind of 'emotional labour' that can occur in such settings. Later, in formal evaluations, both students were able to view the opportunity to explore events from their pasts, both cognitively and emotionally, as helpful in terms of their professional and personal development. This view was echoed by the majority of the other participants.

There are a variety of ways in which nurse educators can facilitate the development of skills in reflection and self-awareness when working with student nurses. That this should be part of the teacher's role seems to be accepted in the majority of curricula underpinning current nurse training. New areas have

---

5. J. Klein, *Our Need for Others and Its Root in Infancy*, Tavistock, London 1987.

been identified for inclusion in mainstream programmes of nurse education; these include reflection and self awareness; the therapeutic use of touch; the therapeutic use of self; and empathic understanding - along with a far greater emphasis on the development of therapeutic nurse patient relationships. All these have great potential for enhancing nursing practice, but also require careful implementation in an educational setting. Issues such as the need for teachers to be skilled in the facilitation of such work, as well as the requirement that those engaged in such activities have access to supervision, may require further consideration. Above all I feel it is vital that what students experience in the classroom is a template for the kind of relationships and associated skills we are teaching, and this includes respecting the students' need for personal space and privacy. Reflection must be voluntary, and when disclosure occurs it must be held with psychological safety for all concerned with the experience.

Miracle on St David's Day

They flash upon that inward eye
Which is the bliss of solitude

The Daffodils, William Wordsworth

An afternoon yellow and open-mouthed
with daffodils. The sun treads the path
among cedars and enormous oaks.
It might be a country house, guests strolling,
the rumps of gardeners between nursery shrubs.

I am reading poetry to the insane.
An old woman, interrupting, offers
as many buckets of coals as I need.
A beautiful chestnut-haired boy listens
entirely absorbed. A schizophrenic

on a good day, they tell me later.
In a cage of first March sun a woman
sits not listening, not seeing, not feeling.
In her neat clothes the woman is absent.
A big mild man is tenderly led

to his chair. He has never spoken.
His labourer's hands on his knees, he rocks
gently to the rhythms of the poems.
I read to their presences, absences,
to the big, dumb labouring man as he rocks.

He is suddenly standing, silently,
huge and mild, but I feel afraid. Like slow
movement of spring water or the first bird
of the year in the breaking darkness,
the labourer's voice recites 'The Daffodils'.

The nurses are frozen, alert; the patients
seem to listen. He is hoarse but word-perfect.
Outside the daffodils are still as wax,
a thousand, ten thousand, their syllables
unspoken, their creams and yellows still.

Forty years ago, in a Valleys school,
the class recited poetry by rote.
Since the dumbness of misery fell
he has remembered there was a music
of speech and that once he had something to say.

When he's done, before the applause, we observe
the flowers' silence. A thrush sings
and the daffodils are aflame.

Gillian Clarke

This poem by Gillian Clarke demonstrates how there are ways other than professional encounters to communicate with patients, even or especially the 'insane'. I heard the poem by chance. It was indeed St David's Day and the poem was part of a radio broadcast to mark the event. I too was frozen, like the nurses, as I heard the description of the labourer dumbed by misery suddenly connecting with 'a music of speech' in the poetry of his childhood. We do not know whether this was a temporary or permanent reprieve, but we do know that an emotional connection was made through the power of poetry. I also wondered about why the man had been silenced for so long and, because it was Wales, I thought it might have been because of the dual deaths of his livelihood as a miner, and of his community.

Pam Smith

'Miracle on St David's Day' was first published in Gillian Clarke's Collected Poems (Carcanet, 1985), and is reprinted here by permission of Carcanet.

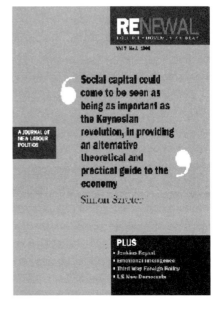

Soundings

Described by the political theorist John Gray as a 'well written and welcome journal', Soundings *is a unique venture that combines hard-edged political argument with a broad spectrum of cultural content. Recent highlights have included Stuart Hall, Jackie Kay, Gail Lewis, Mike Phillips and Lola Young on the significance of* Windrush; *Victoria Brittain and Basil Davidson on states of Africa; Chantal Mouffe on the third way; Angela McRobbie on the culture industries; and Bill Schwarz on the Tories; special themes have also included the European Left, Young Britain, Active Welfare and the Media.*

SPECIAL OFFER TO NEW SUBSCRIBERS

First time individual subscribers are entitled to a £25 subscription for the first year

Subscription rates 1999 (3 issues)

Individual subscriptions: *UK* £35.00 *Rest of the World* £45
Institutional subscriptions: *UK* £70.00 *Rest of the World* £80.00

To subscribe, send your name and address and payment (cheque or credit card), stating which issue you want the subscription to start with, to Soundings, Lawrence and Wishart, 99a Wallis Road, London E9 5LN.
OR you can e-mail us at
subscriptions@l-w-bks.demon.co.uk